THEMES from the MINOR PROPHETS

A Bible Commentary for Laymen
BY DAVID ALLAN HUBBARD

Regal Books A Division of G/L Publications
Ventura, California, U.S.A.

Other good reading in the Bible Commentary for Laymen series:

Highlights of the Bible, Genesis - Nehemiah
  by Ray C. Stedman
Highlights of the Bible, New Testament
  by William F. Lane
Pass It On, I & II Timothy
  by Robert H. Mounce

The foreign language publishing of all Regal books is under the direction of GLINT. GLINT provides financial and technical help for the adaptation, translation and publishing of books in more than 85 languages for millions of people worldwide.

For more information write: GLINT, P.O. Box 6688, Ventura, CA 93006.

Third Printing, 1980

Published by Regal Books
A Division of G/L Publications
Ventura, California 93006
Printed in U.S.A.

Library of Congress Catalog Card No. 74-17861
ISBN 0-8307-0498-1

Contents

A Teacher's Manual and Student Discovery Guide
for use with *Themes from the Minor Prophets*
are available from your church supplier.

Acknowledgments

These chapters began as radio talks on "The Joyful Sound" broadcast. Parts of them were used in the "Thomas Staley Distinguished Christian Scholar Lectures" for 1973 at Northwest Christian College, Eugene, Oregon where I enjoyed the magnanimous hospitality of President Barton A. Dowdy and his colleagues.

My wife, Ruth, has edited and typed most of the manuscript with some assistance from my secretary Marion Matweyiw. Without their help this book could not have appeared.

Introduction

Breathlessly pressing to keep pace with the demands of tomorrow, we men and women who fancy ourselves as modern sometimes think that we have outrun our ancient faith in Scripture. We view the Bible as an old family homestead to be visited occasionally in our attempt to recapture memories of bygone days. But we live somewhere else.

Modern life is too complex, we reason, to yield to the simple solutions of a faith that appeared millennia ago on shores quite foreign to our circumstances. It is to the contemporary disciplines—especially the behavioral sciences like anthropology, psychology, political sciences and sociology—that we sons and daughters of modernity who are rushing into century twenty-one must look.

These disciplines can be of help to us. But we will deceive ourselves beyond correcting if we assume that they have replaced the Bible as a reliable guide to human behavior in its emotional, personal, social and political aspects.

Modern man has some catching up to do. The men and women of the Bible had an experience with God that cannot be outmoded.

The Minor Prophets are a case in point. As we see their messages we will be reminded that the Church has called their writings "Minor" not because they were unimportant, but because they were *brief.* These 12 men whom God chose to bear His Word to His people Israel —and then to us—spoke on topics that read like tomorrow's headlines. Their faith, their insight, their judgment have not been outdistanced by our frantic rush into the future. In fact we will have to stretch to catch up with them.

I have not ventured to give a verse by verse commentary or a running exposition. Rather I have sought to capture a major theme from each prophet and show how it comments on our contemporary predicaments.

"In many and various ways God spoke of old to our fathers by the prophets" (Heb. 1:1). Amid all the welter of voices we are listening to in these turbulent times, we will do ourselves and our world immense good to listen again to them.

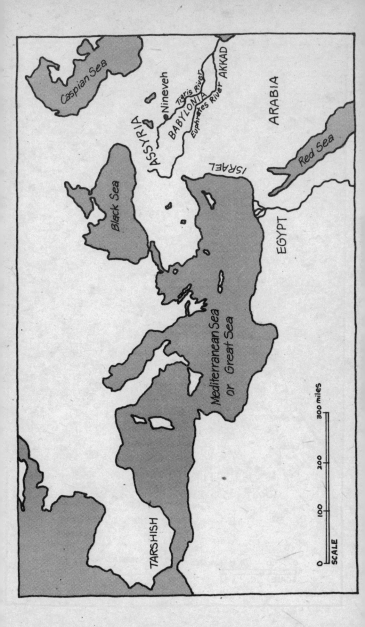

1
Me? Worship Idols?

**Hosea: God Speaks to a People
Seduced by False Gods**

Hosea 11:1,2; 13:1–3
When Israel was a child, I loved him,
  and out of Egypt I called my son.
The more I called them,
  the more they went from me;
they kept sacrificing to the Baals,
  and burning incense to idols.

When Ephraim spoke, men trembled;
  he was exalted in Israel;
but he incurred guilt through
  Baal and died.
And now they sin more and more,
  and make for themselves molten images,
idols skilfully made of their silver,
  all of them the work of craftsmen.
Sacrifice to these, they say.
  Men kiss calves!
Therefore they shall be like the morning mist
  or like the dew that goes early away,
like the chaff that swirls from the
  threshing floor
or like smoke from a window.

Introduction to Hosea

The divided kingdoms of Israel and Judah were on the brink of destruction. God in His mercy sent prophet after prophet to warn His people that if they did not repent and turn to Him they would be doomed. One of these prophets was Hosea, a native of the northern kingdom of Israel.

During the troubled years 750–725 B.C., Hosea was sent by God to confront Israel with her sins of idolatry expressed especially in the worship of Baal, the Canaanite god of fertility. In lyric poetry, with graphic figures of speech, Hosea the prophet pondered Israel's waywardness and God's faithfulness. He tenderly reminded Israel of God's fervent, constant, faithful love. His emphasis on "knowing God" in a relationship of intimacy and obedience was forged in the fires of the prophet's poignant relationship with his wife and family. Hosea's life as well as his words became the vehicle of God's revelation.

Hosea's writings are in two sections: (1) chapters 1:1—3:5, a description of the prophet's marriage to an unfaithful wife as an illustration of the Lord's relationship to Israel who was committing spiritual adultery by worshiping false gods; (2) chapters 4:1—14:9, a series of speeches in which Israel's sins—idolatry, brutality, immorality, ingratitude—are denounced, judgment is threatened, yet restoration is promised.

The name Hosea is related in Hebrew to the name Joshua, which is the Old Testament equivalent to Jesus. Hosea means "salvation." Hosea's preaching did not accomplish its specific purpose: the people did not respond to the message of salvation. The northern kingdom fell to the Assyrians and Shalmaneser V, king of Assyria. Yet in a sense God's larger purpose through Hosea has been accomplished: generations of God's people have been reminded of His relentless love. Hosea's cross of tragic suffering and bitter rejection has helped us all to understand and appreciate that later cross by which God has brought salvation to all who believe.

Idolatry is the human problem, whether ancient or modern. The human imagination is a factory tooled to produce false images of God.

These images are not just the idle fantasies we frequently engage in. They are not merely our Walter Mitty dreams of fame, success, and recognition.

They are much more basic and much more dangerous —our false images of God. They are more basic because none of us lives without them. Each of us has ideas about what is holy and what is majestic for us. Each of us has ideas or ideals that we consider too sacred to be tampered with, too precious to be laughed at.

You will never meet a person who is not religious. Not that everyone goes to church, studies religious books, or faithfully carries out religious rituals. But even the most secular of modern persons has a reverence for something beyond himself. Business success, political power, financial gain, intellectual prowess, material comfort, sensual pleasure are just a few of the ambitions that people are willing to devote themselves to.

Measure a person's use of time, weigh the attention given to various topics in conversation and you will get a picture of what that person worships.

Such worship is dangerous. It crowds the true and living God out of our lives. Or even worse it makes Him the tool by which we try to achieve the ambition that is our real god. We ask God to support our national causes, because patriotism has become our idol. We beg God to help us succeed financially, because money is what we really worship.

Such worship is dangerous. It degrades the worshiper. It pins his hopes on things that are not helpful. It builds his life on things that are not fundamental. It anchors his mind to things that are not permanent.

Our idolatry is so ingrained that it takes shocking, almost brutal tactics to call it to our attention. One of the ministries of the Bible is to use such tactics to jerk us up short and force us to see what we are really doing when we worship something besides the God of the Bible. With biting irony the prophet Hosea did this:

> And now they sin more and more,
>> and make for themselves molten images,
> idols skilfully made of their silver,
>> all of them the work of craftsmen.
> Sacrifice to these, they say.
> Men kiss calves! (Hos. 13:2)

"Men kiss calves!" That says it all. Our idols are like the golden calves built at Bethel and other shrines in Israel. Originally they were intended to be footstools for the God of Israel, but quickly they came to be revered in themselves. Baal, the Canaanite god of fertility, was often pictured as a bull, so the connection between the calf and Baal worship was readily made. And, apparently, part of the ritual of adoration was to kiss the golden image.

"Men kiss calves!" We adore what we outrank. We worship what was made to serve us. And when we do we lower ourselves to the status of things or animals.

14

Men and women were made to glorify God, not to kiss calves.

The Bible helps us to learn this in two obvious ways. It teaches us how far astray we have gone. And it pictures for us clearly and repeatedly the power, grace, and glory of the living God. Modern man will do well to catch up with the Bible on both these points.

Sometimes we think of the God of the Old Testament as a God only of wrath. We are apt to carry a picture of sharp contrasts in our minds between the God of the Old Testament, holy and majestic, and the God of the New, gracious and loving. Much of the Old Testament has to be overlooked if this type of contrast is to be made, because the God of the Bible is one God—loving and righteous, gracious and wrathful, eager to draw people to Himself and judging them when they refuse to be drawn.

Nowhere in the Old Testament is the gracious, kind, loving character of God seen so clearly as in the book of Hosea. Modern man in his quest for a true understanding of the nature of God can scarcely do better than to look at Hosea's experiences and especially at Hosea's God.

Hosea lived in the days of Jeroboam II, son of Joash, who reigned for about 40 years and died about 750 B.C. This was Israel's golden age, the most splendid and influential period in the history of the northern kingdom. Her fortress capital at Samaria was lavishly decorated with imported ivory. Her wealthy leaders rested complacently in the lap of luxury. This was her golden age—in military power, in political influence, in economic stability. Yet, as Amos, the other great prophet of the northern kingdom, noted, she was rotten to the core.

She had turned her back on the one thing that made her unique as a people—her faith in the God who had redeemed her. It was at this period—this time of luxurious degradation, of splendor and shame, of military might and religious corruption—that God spoke to Hosea and called him to be a prophet. No ordinary prophet was Hosea to be, for God called him not only to *preach* but to *live* his message.

Israel's Harlotry

Hosea dates the beginning of his prophetic ministry, which probably followed Amos' by a decade or two, to the time when God commanded him to marry a woman who was to be untrue to him and to bear children who shared her impurity (see Hos. 1:2). The purpose of this command was clear: Hosea's marriage to the unfaithful Gomer was to be a demonstration of God's relationship to Israel, His people. God Himself gives the reason for the command: "For the land commits great harlotry by forsaking the LORD" (Hos. 1:2).

In the exodus from Egypt God had entered into a special relationship with Israel, which is called a *covenant.* In response to what God had done in saving His people, in leading them through the sea and across the desert, they pledged themselves to be His people, His bride. Their vow to Him was like a marriage vow—they solemnly swore to be faithful and obedient to Him forever: "And all the people answered with one voice, and said, 'All the words which the LORD has spoken we will do'" (Exod. 24:3).

But when they entered the Promised Land, they found their vows difficult to keep. The Canaanites had a very different approach to religion—they worshiped

Baal, not the Lord. To Baal or the Baals they attributed their crops and flocks. The plural is sometimes used to indicate that Baal had different manifestations of himself in different regions of the land. As god of fertility, Baal (the name means *master* or *lord*) was responsible for the cycles of the seasons. The Israelites began to pray and to sacrifice to him and to thank him for the blessings of the land:

> When Israel was a child, I loved him,
>   and out of Egypt I called my son.
> The more I called them,
>   the more they went from me;
> they kept sacrificing to the Baals,
>   and burning incense to idols (Hos. 11:1,2).

This worship of Baal was unfaithfulness to the Lord—a kind of spiritual harlotry, an act of playing false with her true husband:

> For their mother has played the harlot;
>   she that conceived them has acted shamefully.
> For she said, "I will go after my lovers,
>   who give me my bread and my water,
>   my wool and my flax, my oil and
>   my drink" (Hos. 2:5).

The mother of Hosea's children, in her adultery, illustrated Israel's waywardness. Israel's lovers were the Canaanite gods who, by their pagan ceremonies, which included immorality and drunkenness, had lured Israel away from her true husband—the Lord who had redeemed her. "Men kissed calves!"

God's Judgment

At this point God had no choice but to judge. He had

to drive His people to their knees in order to draw them back to Himself:

> Therefore I will hedge up her way
>> with thorns;
> and I will build a wall against her,
>> so that she cannot find her paths.
> She shall pursue her lovers,
>> but not overtake them;
> and she shall seek them,
>> but shall not find them.
> Then she shall say, "I will go
>> and return to my first husband,
>> for it was better with me then
>>> than now" (Hos. 2:6,7).

The very names of the children born to Gomer, Hosea's wife, describe the judgment of God. The oldest son was named *Jezreel:* "God shall scatter." Next a daughter came along whom Hosea named *Lo-Ruhamah:* "Not pitied, for I will no more have pity on the house of Israel, to forgive them at all." Then another son joined the family. *Lo Ammi* Hosea called him: "Not my people" (Hos. 1:4–9).

Together these three names are a terrible description of God's wrath upon His people: *Jezreel,* God shall scatter them in judgment and that judgment will take place in the valley of Jezreel, the great plain that cuts across the heart of Israel; *Lo-Ruhamah,* He shall no longer pour out His pity upon them; *Lo Ammi,* they are no more His covenant people. Hosea's marriage and Hosea's family had become object lessons of the impurity and corruption of Israel—symbolized by Gomer's unfaithfulness—and of the stern judgment of God—illustrated in the names of the children themselves. Whoever called those three youngsters by name must have been reminded that the God of Israel was about to divorce His people on grounds of infidelity.

God's Forgiveness

But this judgment is not God's last word to Israel or to Hosea. Judgment there would be and plenty of it. Israel was to be stripped of her possessions, her crops, her religious festivities, and her land:

> Therefore I will take back my grain in its time,
> and my wine in its season;
> and I will take away my wool and my flax,
> which were to cover her nakedness.
> Now I will uncover her lewdness in the sight of
> her lovers, and no one shall rescue her out
> of my hand.
> And I will put an end to all her mirth, her
> feasts, her new moons, her sabbaths, and
> all her appointed feasts.
> And I will lay waste her vines and her fig trees,
> of which she said,
> "These are my hire, which my lovers have
> given me."
> I will make them a forest, and the beasts of the
> field shall devour them.
> And I will punish her for the feast days of the
> Baals when she burned incense to them
> and decked herself with her ring and jewelry,
> and went after her lovers, and forgot me,
> says the LORD (Hos. 2:9–13).

But beyond the judgment lies forgiveness—God refused to give up His people and chose rather to draw them back to Himself. Hosea's very language catches us by surprise. The announcement of judgment was so dour that we are not prepared for what God said next:

> Therefore, behold, I will allure her,
>> and bring her into the wilderness,
>> and speak tenderly to her.
> And there I will give her her vineyards,
>> and make the Valley of Achor a door of hope.
> And there she shall answer as in the days of
>> her youth,
>> as at the time when she came out of
>> the land of Egypt (Hos. 2:14,15).

In other words a new exodus is to take place: God will again meet His people in the desert and assure them of His love; God will turn the Valley of Achor, where Israel had such trouble in the days of Achan (see Josh. 7), into a doorway of hope.

More than that, He will wipe out the memory of the false lovers:

> And in that day, says the LORD, you
> will call me, "My husband," and no
> longer will you call me, "My Baal."
> For I will remove the names of the
> Baals from her mouth, and they shall
> be mentioned by name no more
> (Hos. 2:16,17).

> And I will betroth you to me for ever;
> I will betroth you to me in righteousness
> and in justice, in steadfast love, and in
> mercy. I will betroth you to me in faithfulness;
> and you shall know the LORD
> (Hos. 2:19,20).

God will forgive; He will restore; He will bless. The

true and living God will woo and win His people. When His love and grace are clearly seen, the Baals look cheap, tawdry, and impotent by comparison.

Israel's new marriage, her return to fellowship, will bring a new day. God will reverse His previous judgments. He does this in a play on the names of Hosea's children. Names that ring of judgment will be changed to sound the call of forgiveness:

> And in that day, says the LORD,
> I will answer the heavens
> and they shall answer the earth;
> and the earth shall answer the grain,
> the wine, and the oil,
> and they shall answer Jezreel;
> and I will sow him for myself in
> the land.
> And I will have pity on Not pitied,
> and I will say to Not my people,
> "You are my people";
> and he shall say, "Thou art my
> God" (Hos. 2:21–23).

Heaven and earth will combine, at the command of God, to bless the land. Scattered Israel will be replanted by God; separated Israel will be reconciled to God; alienated Israel will be refreshed by God's mercy.

Hosea's Response

The story does not end here. It returns to where it began—Hosea's relationship to Gomer. God commanded the prophet to take again the faithless wife and live with her:

> And the LORD said to me, "Go again,
> love a woman who is beloved of a

> paramour and is an adulteress; even
> as the LORD loves the people of
> Israel, though they turn to other gods
> and love cakes of raisins." So I bought
> her for fifteen shekels of silver and
> a homer and a lethech of barley. And
> I said to her, "You must dwell as mine
> for many days; you shall not play the
> harlot, or belong to another man; so
> will I also be to you" (Hos. 3:1–3).

God urged Hosea to become an object lesson of forgiving grace, to demonstrate in His own experience the love of God who loved to the uttermost. We can guess how hard this must have been for the prophet—yet he did it. He had gained a fresh vision of the love of God, and from it had learned to forgive.

If the idolatries of modern man are to be exposed as frauds, God may use us as part of that exposé. Hosea was called upon to demonstrate concretely how much God suffers when human beings play false with Him. Hosea was also called to dramatize the grace and love which reach out to all of us idolaters in the midst of our spiritual harlotry.

What a compelling picture of our God Hosea gives us. Refusing to let judgment be the last word He makes every effort to bring us to Himself. His heart is broken by our sin and rebellion—yet He goes on loving, why? Hosea gives the answer in chapter 11, verse 9, "I am God and not man." His love is boundless, His grace knows no measure.

What Hosea's tragic experience taught him about God's love many another has learned. It never fails. There is no sin so great that He cannot forgive it, no stain so dark that He cannot remove it, no plight so desperate that he cannot remedy it, no sinner so far removed that He cannot draw him to Himself. Hosea's God is John's God—faithful and just to forgive. He is Paul's God—forgiving, kind, tenderhearted. He is the God and Father of Jesus Christ—who came not to call the righteous but sinners to repentance.

Have you taken this God as your God? Have you renounced your idolatry? Have you stopped kissing calves? Have you asked Him to forgive you? Have you confessed your rebellion to Him? Have you found in your own experience the joy of knowing that the God of all heaven and earth loves you and longs for you to turn to Him? If you have done this, you are not alone. Many modern men and women have turned to this God from their idols and have begun to catch up with the Bible.

Prayer: Our Father, we can call you that with greater warmth and finer confidence now that we know how you stand by us. Keep the picture of your living presence and your loving power so clear before us that we will fix our attention on you at all times. Expose the ugliness of our idolatry for the revolting relationship it really is, and teach us to worship you with all we are and have. In Jesus' name. Amen.

2
Just Why Do So Many Things Go Wrong?

Joel: God Speaks to a World Torn by Calamity

Joel 2:26–29
You shall eat in plenty and be satisfied,
  and praise the name of the LORD your God,
 who has dealt wondrously with you.
And my people shall never again be put to shame.
You shall know that I am in the midst of Israel,
  and that I, the LORD, am your God and there is
    none else.
And my people shall never again be put to shame.
And it shall come to pass afterward,
  that I will pour out my spirit on all flesh;
your sons and your daughters shall prophesy,
  your old men shall dream dreams, and your young
    men shall see visions.
Even upon the menservants and maidservants
in those days, I will pour out my spirit.

Introduction to Joel

"Has such a thing happened in your days, or in the days of your fathers?" (1:2). With these words the prophet Joel began his plea to God's people to heed the divine warning of a great calamity that had befallen the land.

Although scholars are uncertain about the date of Joel's writing—opinions vary from 800–400 B.C.—the message is as relevant to God's people today as it was when it was first written. Joel calls on us to remember our need for repentance before the "Day of the Lord"—the day of God's judgment—comes upon us. Although Joel gives us no personal information (other than that he was the son of Penuel) and no historical references such as the names of kings of any of the nations, the attention he pays to the Temple and its offerings suggest that Joel lived in Judah, perhaps in Jerusalem.

In vivid, imaginative poetry he describes a catastrophic invasion of locusts that descended upon various sectors of the population (1:1—2:17). He cries to the people to repent. Then he prophesies the coming victory in which the plague's damage is restored, God's Spirit is outpoured, nations are judged and Judah is rescued (2:18—3:21).

The headlines shriek their terrifying news. Letters two inches high shout their tragic message. Almost weekly in some part of the world it happens. Calamity.

A dark, funnel-shaped cloud comes snarling out of the sky. Churning and biting, dipping and whirling it seems to suck the very life out of places it touches. Roofs are lifted, cars are overturned, walls are collapsed, windows are shattered, their fragments sprayed like bullets. "TORNADO KILLS FOUR IN KANSAS TOWN" the headline reads. Calamity.

Rains swamp the coastline with the force of a hundred waterfalls. Roaring winds bend palm trees double. Whipped into a white fury the sea ravages the shore. It is that season of the year, and the headlines herald it: "MONSOON HITS INDIAN COAST—THOUSANDS HOMELESS." Calamity.

Rescue workers dig frantically. Drifting snow slaps at their faces. Frost bites through their gloves and caps. Their breath freezes on their beards as they labor. Alertly they listen for cough or cry, tap or moan. They are still in shock as they relive the horror of the angry roar, the sharp crunching of the ice, the shattering of the silence of the Alpine night. The headlines of the world spread the dreadful message: "AVALANCHE BURIES SWISS TOWN—HUNDREDS FEARED DEAD." Calamity.

Helicopters whirr overhead, and their crews broadcast on-the-spot reports. "The crack in the dam seems to be widening. The roads are jammed as the families that live below the dam evacuate their homes leaving their belongings behind. Now we are flying over the pile of rubble that was once the wing of a hospital. Ambulances line the streets, and we can see the stretcher-bearers carrying the survivors to safety. The whole neighborhood is a shambles—houses cracked wide open, vast fissures in the streets, ruptured water mains spouting like geysers, churches with crumbled steeples, confused people staring emptily or scurrying aimlessly in the streets. California's worst earthquake in 30 years." Calamity.

Year after year through the centuries of our history, our world has been torn by calamity. Events over which man has no control whatever threaten to crush his spirit and snuff out his life. And a lot more than physical hurt is involved. When the rubble has been cleared, the dead buried, and the wounded given aid and comfort, the nagging, burning questions begin to take their toll: Why? Why this way? Why here? Why us? Why now? When again? Should we leave? Where would we go?

Modern man has made little progress in answering questions like these. He sometimes has a little more warning about cyclone or hurricane. He can study earthquake faults and measure the pressures pent up beneath the earth's surface. He builds stronger structures to resist the blowing and shaking. But he can no more ward off hurricane or quake than could his less enlightened ancestors. Nor can he find ready answers to the puzzles that have perplexed people throughout history when they have mused on the meaning of calamity.

Once again the biblical prophets offer some help. One book of the Old Testament has calamity as its main subject. If newspapers had existed in the days of the prophet Joel, their headlines would have read something like this: "INSECT PLAGUE WIPES OUT CROPS." And the story would have included the following description: "An invasion of locusts ravaged the land of Israel this week leaving no green thing alive. The thoroughness and savagery of the insect army was beyond any similar invasion in the memory of the oldest citizens of the land. As an eyewitness put it:

What the cutting locust left,
    the swarming locust has eaten.
What the swarming locust left,

> the hopping locust has eaten,
>   and what the hopping locust left,
>   the destroying locust has eaten (Joel 1:4).

"Wave after wave of insects have attacked the foliage, laying waste the grape vines, splintering the fig trees, stripping their bark and leaving their branches white, blanched in the middle-eastern sun. Palm, apple and pomegranate trees are all withered, as are the fields of wheat and barley. The plague has created a religious crisis as well, because the priests have no food or drink for their daily offerings in the Temple."

Of course the newspaper part is imaginary, but that description of the plague follows closely what Joel reports in the first chapter of his book. A calamity of no mean proportion had struck his land, and the prophet was called by God to help the people cope with it. Two lessons he has passed along that a world torn by calamity can do well to heed: how to learn from calamity and how to live with calamity.

How to Learn from Calamity

Calamity is almost impossible to interpret. But that does not stop us from trying. Some people view calamity as chance, accident, mishap. They see it as one of the mysteries of life over which we have no control and in which we can find no meaning. "Too bad," they say, "but I guess that's just the way life is."

Others explain calamity on purely natural terms. When certain physical conditions exist, nature works a certain way. A combination of hot and cold air creates high- and low-pressure areas which cause strong winds. Atmospheric conditions may produce unusual amounts of snow which in turn leads to flooding in the spring.

Still others view calamity as demonic, a display of the power of Satan. They read it as a victory for the forces of evil in the age-long struggle between God and His enemies.

And there may be elements of truth in all these interpretations. Life *is* like that. Bad things do just seem to happen. And usually they happen in accordance with natural principles. Satan, too, may be at work, not so much in the disaster itself as in our response to it. He may work on our fears, encourage our bitterness, feed our confusion, contribute to our despair.

The Bible looks on calamity another way. What we call natural disaster, it calls the work of God. Our insurance policies have picked this up better than most of us have. They call hurricane, flood, earthquake "acts of God." Take Joel's locust plague, for instance. Because the people recognized that God, in some way, was at work they learned valuable lessons from their calamity.

They learned *something about the provision of God.* Crops they had taken for granted they were now denied. Food for which they had not truly been grateful they now missed sorely. What the Lord had once given He now took away. And they began to realize who it was who had provided for their daily care.

> Unto thee, O LORD, I cry.
> For fire has devoured the pastures of the
>   wilderness,
> and flame has burned
>   all the trees of the field.
> Even the wild beasts cry to thee
>   because the water brooks are dried up
>   (Joel 1:19,20).

Man and beast both acknowledge God's provision.

What a pity that we have to wait until God's provision is cut off before we show gratitude. But this is one thing calamity can teach us.

From the locust attack Joel's countrymen also learned *something about the power of God.* The Lord who gave could take away. His blessings were not to be taken lightly. His grace was not to be tampered with. Where these cautions were ignored, His power showed itself in judgment.

God takes full responsibility for the locust invasion. His power is at work in the insect army. They move at His command:

> The LORD utters his voice
>   before his army,
> for his host is exceedingly great;
>   he that executes his word is powerful.
> For the day of the LORD is great and
>   very terrible;
>   who can endure it? (Joel 2:11).

A horde of insects is described as "the day of the Lord." God is not beyond using bugs or anything else to teach us lessons of His provision and power. A lot of things He has designed for our comfort in life, but He is not embarrassed to make us terribly uncomfortable when we need to learn more about Him. Our character means more to Him than our comfort, and lessons learned in calamity are one means of maturing our character.

How to Live with Calamity

Learning from calamity is one thing. Living with calamity is another. We cannot stave it off or ignore it. Calamity will come. When it does, we can learn lessons

31

of God's provision and power. That's good. But we still have to live with the hardship and heartache that calamity triggers.

One way we do this is to *hold to the hope of restoration.* God is not through with our spinning globe, even though He blasts it and shakes it from time to time. To people rocked by disaster His words of invitation hold out hope:

> "Yet even now," says the LORD,
> > "return to me with all your heart,
> with fasting, with weeping, and with mourning;
> > and rend your hearts and not your gar
> > ments."
> Return to the LORD, your God,
> > for he is gracious and merciful,
> slow to anger, and abounding in steadfast love,
> > and repents of evil (Joel 2:12,13).

Acts of compassion, not calamity, are what God is best known for. Returning to Him always leads to life. Even when it looks as though He is set against us, our change of heart will move Him to change His ways. Bank on His mercy even when life seems merciless, and see what happens.

Another way we learn to live with calamity is to *believe the promise of the Spirit.* God has high plans for our planet, plans He first announced to Joel centuries before Christ:

> And it shall come to pass afterward,
> > that I will pour out my spirit on all flesh;
> your sons and your daughters shall prophesy,
> > your old men shall dream dreams, and your
> > young men shall see visions.
> Even upon the menservants and maidservants

in those days, I will pour out my spirit
(Joel 2:28,29).

All flesh, both sexes, all ages, all classes—God's Spirit. Think of it. What begins with a terrifying picture of judgment—a locust plague—ends with a comforting promise of a worldwide work of God in power and blessing through His Spirit.

When Jesus Christ formed His Church at Pentecost He started this prophecy on its way to fulfillment. Now around the world God has His people, called by His name, forgiven by His grace, empowered by His Spirit. God is at work everywhere to draw people to Him.

Calamities there may be (and we don't want them or like them), but like a great signpost lifting its message above the calamity is God's promise: I am not done with this aging earth; I am making its citizens new by the power of my Spirit. Not an army of locusts, but wave after wave, group after group of God's people is His new invasion force. Not disaster but health and healing march with them.

I hope calamity stays away from your door until Jesus comes again and Joel's great words of hope, restoration and power are fulfilled to the letter. But if it does come (and modern man has felt its bite as keenly as his ancient forebears), be ready. Catch up with the Bible. Calamity or no, His love can see you through.

Prayer: Father, we don't want calamity at all. We ask you to keep it away from us and to protect us if it comes. But above all help us to trust you. You are doing great things through the wonder of your forgiveness and the power of your Spirit. Include us in these great things, for Jesus' sake. Amen.

3
Why Can't I Worship God My Own Way?

Amos: God Speaks to an Age Turned Sentimental

Amos 3:2; 5:21–24; 9:7
"You only have I known
of all the families of the earth;
therefore I will punish you
for all your iniquities.

"I hate, I despise your feasts,
and I take no delight in your
solemn assemblies.
Even though you offer me your burnt
offerings and cereal offerings,
I will not accept them,
and the peace offerings of your fatted beasts
I will not look upon.
Take away from me the noise of your songs;
to the melody of your harps I will not listen.
But let justice roll down like waters, and
righteousness like an everflowing stream.

"Are you not like the Ethiopians to me,
O people of Israel?" says the LORD.
"Did I not bring up Israel from the land of Egypt,
and the Philistines from Caphtor and the
Syrians from Kir?"

Introduction to Amos

Amos, a sheep rancher and dresser of sycamore (fig) trees, was following his flock in the hills and pastures around his hometown of Tekoa, in the southern kingdom of Judah. One day, around the year 760 B.C., the word of the Lord roared from Zion, and sent Amos, who was neither a "prophet nor a prophet's son" (7:14) to the northern kingdom of Israel.

Straight into Bethel "the king's sanctuary" (7:13) Amos took God's warning to the people. The Lord had judged Israel's neighbors—Damascus, Gaza, Tyre, Edom, Ammon, Moab, and Judah—for inhumanity against one another (1:1 —2:5). The Lord had judged Israel for disregarding God's covenant, ignoring God's warnings and oppressing the poor (2:6—5:17). The Lord said, "Woe to you" who luxuriate in God's blessings at the expense of the poor (5:18—6:14). The Lord gave Amos visions of judgment, showing the coming destruction, its immediacy, the reasons for it, and God's personal involvement in it (7:1—9:10).

But then, in His great love, God promised restoration for Israel after His great judgment. He promised to raise up, to repair, to rebuild, to restore and to replant His people in the land He had given them (9:11–15).

The book of Amos is written in a polished yet powerful literary style. The prophecy shows a moral and spiritual intensity in its grasp of the meaning of God's holiness and righteousness, and flashes out against sin in every form. The prophet writes in a tone of doom in view of the inevitability of judgment. Amos emphasizes God's universal sovereignty which extends to nations far beyond the boundaries of Israel. He portrays the force with which God's call came to Israel's great prophets (3:1–7).

Our generation is shoving God to the margin of life. We are crowding Him out of the center of our lives and leaving the edges to Him. We want Him around when it is useful to us, but we do not want Him intruding when it is not. Maybe He is like a butler at a party who stands silently against the wall until his hostess needs him and beckons him with her eye to bring more gravy or clear the dishes. Or maybe we treat God like the relief pitcher in the bullpen who stays out of sight until the team gets in bad trouble—say, bases loaded and nobody out—then we call him in.

We want God when we feel like it. *Feel* is the key word today. We pray if we feel like it. We obey God when we feel like it. We are governed and guided by feelings. Sentimental we might call ourselves—citizens of a sentimental age. We shape and reshape God by our feelings, changing His standards to fit our own, tailoring His character to suit our needs. We have reversed the process of creation and made God in our own image. But the character of God is not up for grabs. His words and His ways are not like putty that can be shaped in any fashion we deem right.

The Hebrew prophets knew better, and we in our sentimental generation would do well to listen to them. We today are tempted to speculate about God. But the prophets knew Him. They belonged to a people with whom God had daily dealings. And they were uniquely called to serve Him. In many ways, modern men and women have not yet caught up with them.

Usually the prophets were not specially trained; they had other jobs. But God had shown Himself to them in compelling ways. Moses' attention was captured by the burning bush. Isaiah was arrested by the vision of God in the Temple. Jeremiah was drafted as a young man. And Amos was a sheep rancher and orchard grower.

Amos lived in Tekoa, southeast of Bethlehem, not far from the Dead Sea, and probably raised flocks of sheep for Temple sacrifices. We should not picture him as a peasant farmer or hired man but more likely as an educated landowner, as his knowledge of history and his skill in speaking suggest. But Amos' distinction is not so much in his background as in his sense of call and his dedication to that call. He did not volunteer; he was drafted. As he puts it, when a lion roars unexpectedly, we cannot help but be afraid. When God speaks, we cannot help but prophesy. (See Amos 3:8.)

Amos' view of God is important but not complete, because no prophet says everything about God. Each sketches aspects of His character; no one says it all. In fact, we have to look at the New Testament to see the full picture of God. In Jesus Christ, all God's fullness dwells in bodily form. Amos does not say everything, still he does say some things about God that our age desperately needs to hear.

Amos speaks of a God who rules all nations, who governs the march of history and yet gives Himself in love in a special way to His people. He is God of the nations and Lord of Israel, the God of righteousness and justice, who calls us into a vital, meaningful relationship with Him.

God's Knowledge of Our Problems

It is always amazing to see how up-to-date God's Word is and how contemporary are the problems it comments on. And why shouldn't it be? God knows the end from the beginning and He knows everything in between, too. Human nature doesn't change a great deal. What God moved men to write 2700 years ago can have telling relevance.

Look at some of our chief problems today and then hear what Amos the prophet has to say.

False confidence in military might (Amos 2:14–15):
> Flight shall perish from the swift, and
>   the strong shall not retain his strength,
>   nor shall the mighty save his life;
> he who handles the bow shall not stand,
> and he who is swift of foot shall not
>   save himself,
> nor shall he who rides the horse
>   save his life.

A selfish, wicked use of power (Amos 1:13):
> Thus says the LORD:
> "For three transgressions of the Ammonites,
>   and for four, I will not revoke the
>   punishment;
> because they have ripped up women
>   with child in Gilead,
>   that they might enlarge their border."

Wealth without a sense of compassion and responsibility (Amos 6:4–6):
> Woe to those who lie upon beds of ivory,
> and stretch themselves upon their couches,
> and eat lambs from the flock,
>   and calves from the midst of the stall;
> who sing idle songs to the sound of the harp,
>   and like David invent for themselves

instruments of music;
who drink wine in bowls,
and anoint themselves with the finest oils,
but are not grieved over the ruin of Joseph!
Religious ritual without a concern for true righteousness
(Amos 5:21,24):
I hate, I despise your feasts,
and I take no delight in your
solemn assemblies.
But let justice roll down like waters,
and righteousness like an everflowing stream.

The basic problems have not really changed, and God's attitude toward them surely is constant and consistent. We may feel that things are different now—that we can ignore God's way and go unscathed—but that is a mistake of our sentimental age.

Our *feelings* about God are important. We are to love, worship and serve Him. But we cannot let our feelings determine what He is like. We must let Him tell us through His prophets like Amos.

Amos preached in about 760 B.C. during a time of great peace and prosperity in Israel. Amos belonged to Judah, yet his preaching is leveled at the people of Samaria. He probably got to know them on business trips and was shocked at the disregard of the commandments that God had given Israel in the beginning.

God's Universal Sovereignty

Israel thought God's covenant with them shut Him off from other nations. But Amos said, "not at all." In fact, he begins his book by showing that even Israel's enemies are God's concern. Damascus, proud capital of Syria, Gaza and other great Philistine cities like Ashdod, Ashkelon and Ekron, Tyre on the Phoenician coast and Edom to the south, Moab and Ammon to the east, all are accountable to God. They may ignore God but they have to reckon with Him. He holds them responsible for their acts toward other peoples.

Notice the kinds of crimes for which God promises judgment—breaking treaties, handling the people of Gilead with cruelty, selling men and women into slavery, desecrating the body of the king of Edom—all brazen acts of inhumanity, often connected with war and conquest.

In each case God threatens to send fire to destroy the strongholds of the nations. Judgment was demanded. The foreign nations had not lived up to their own standards, let alone to God's. And judgment was *possible* because the mighty God was ruler of all nations.

God's Covenant Love

And yet He was specially, peculiarly related to Israel, as Amos reminded them. God had brought them out of Egypt and settled them in their land (Amos 2:9–11). He had given them the Law—a special privilege and responsibility. Notice that when God turns from the nations to speak to Judah and Israel, His own people, He judges them by the Law which He had given, not by the general law of human decency that He uses with the nations.

The most important verse in Amos describing God's relationship to Israel is 3:2:

> You only have I known
>   of all the families of the earth;

41

> therefore I will punish you
> for all your iniquities.

God's special grace, His personal and constant care for Israel, carries with it weighty responsibility. Israel was called by God to be a servant. Duty not comfort should have been his motto, service not pleasure his watchword. Israel's role for God was like our idea of a public servant. Think of what we ask of our presidents— their time, their energy, sometimes their very lives. They are our servants—privileged, yes, but also responsible.

Now the lessons learned from Amos' words about Israel and the nations are obvious. The first is that *great privilege carries great responsibility.* God cared in general for the nations, provided their support and guided their overall destiny. And He required that they act humanely and decently toward others. But Israel, whom He had called to Himself with special love and care, also bore greater responsibility in keeping the law and obeying God in every way. She had more light from God and so suffered greater judgment when she failed.

The second lesson is that, though God is Lord of all history, King of all the nations, *He worked out His special purposes in Israel*—demonstrating love, preserving the Scriptures, preparing for the coming of Christ. And the situation is the same today. The destinies of all the nations—whatever race or political structure—are in God's hand. Yet He works specially through His people, who are called to serve Him.

What a word for a sentimental age! God is not dependent on our feelings. *He is.* He rules all nations. He gives Himself in love to all who trust Him and accept what He has done for us in Jesus Christ.

42

God's Righteous Demands

As human beings we tend to deal with God in two speeds: We ignore Him and brush Him aside, or reshape Him and make Him soft and pliable. Either way we end up with a God whom we can conveniently forget about. The prophets tried to show that we cannot ignore God and that we cannot reckon with Him on our own terms, only on His.

The people of Israel had thought that their covenant made them such a favorite of God that nothing could happen to them. Amos warned that they had misunderstood the nature of God's judgment and the meaning of the day of the Lord:

> Woe to you who desire the day of the LORD!
> > Why would you have the day of the LORD?
> It is darkness, and not light (Amos 5:18).

Israel had thought it was the time of special blessing and happiness for her. But Amos says:

> As if a man fled from a lion,
> and a bear met him;
> or went into the house and leaned
> > with his hand against the wall,
> and a serpent bit him.
> Is not the day of the LORD darkness,
> > and not light,
> > and gloom with no brightness in it?
> > (Amos 5:19,20).

A former student of Fuller Seminary was taking a walk in the hills of Pasadena one hot summer day. He wanted to find a place to rest and meditate and pray. He saw a ledge and thought he could pull himself up on it.

As he put his fingers up on the ledge he felt a sting on his hand and dropped down to realize that he had been bitten by a rattlesnake. The site that he thought was to be his place of composure and meditation very nearly became the scene of his death.

This is an illustration of the nature of the day of the Lord. The Israelites thought it would be peace and security. But God said it is going to be ripe with judgment, because Israel's was an empty religion:

> I hate, I despise your feasts,
>> and I take no delight in your solemn assemblies.
> Even though you offer me your burnt
>> offerings and cereal offerings,
> I will not accept them,
> and the peace offerings of your fatted beasts
> I will not look upon.
> Take away from me the noise of your songs;
>> to the melody of your harps I will not listen.
> But let justice roll down like waters,
>> and righteousness like an everflowing
>> stream (Amos 5:21–24).

It is not empty religion, it is not hollow ritual that pleases God, but justice and righteousness—like mighty streams washing away corruption, bringing the life and refreshment that God covets for His people.

Righteousness means primarily a right relationship with God. Justice speaks of a compassionate integrity. Righteousness suggests that we stick by God's standards, and justice insists that we do the right thing toward others for the right reasons.

The background for these concepts, righteousness and justice, is the covenant that God made with His people when He brought them out of the land of Egypt. He had played the gods of Egypt on their own court and whipped them soundly. And then He said to Israel, "I am the Lord your God who brought you out of the land of Egypt. . . . You shall have no other gods before me" (Exod. 20:2,3). He demanded their religious loyalty and insisted on social justice as part of the covenant pattern. He talked about not stealing, not coveting, safeguarding the neighbors' property, not bearing false witness in court against a neighbor.

Religious loyalty or righteousness means *maintaining a right relationship to God*. Now what does this involve as the prophet Amos sees it? It involves *rejecting idolatry*. The reason why the Hebrew prophets were so dead set against idolatry was that idolatry is always misleading. Whatever form you picture God in will lead you away from God rather than toward Him. A sun god, a winged lion, a coiled snake on a stick—all the forms the ancients used to depict their gods were deceptive lies according to the prophet.

This religious loyalty also means *taking the gap between us and God with full seriousness*. It means realizing that He is God and we are not. Therefore, we have to repent and we have to receive the grace of God. The relationship is established as His gift, not as our achievement. It comes because of His grace, not because of our success.

But there is something else to see. True righteousness means *becoming like the One we worship*. Conforming to His standard is part of it. God wants us to do what is right, and He has standards that we have to measure up to.

When I was in junior high school I took woodshop.

One of our projects was to make a game board. We were given a board that was six and one-half inches square. Then we were told to plane this board down to six inches and to have the edges level and square. When I got one edge right long-ways it was wrong crossways, and I kept cutting that board smaller and smaller without getting it square. Every time I thought it was right, the righteous standard—the square—would tell me it was wrong. Our grade was determined by the size of the game board. If it was six inches square, we got an A; if it was five inches square we got a B; if it was four inches, we got a C. When I finished I had the only pin-on game board in the school! As my work was called into question constantly by the square, so God judges our lives by His standards.

But more than that is involved. We are to *grow into His likeness* just as friend makes an impact on friend. As children speak, walk, talk and think the way their parents do, so God's character leaves its mark on us when we make personal commitment to Him.

We are called, if we are really to be righteous, to *resist empty religion*. We are not just going through the motions when we sing hymns and say prayers. We want to put our hearts and spirits into what we do. We seek the full meaning of the form in which we worship. And we do not want to lose the spirit of worship in its structure.

Since God takes Himself seriously, we must. There is no game playing—no tampering or trifling with God. He is a *God of righteousness*. And Amos says, "Let righteousness roll down like an everflowing stream."

But God is also the *God of justice*, the God who expects passionate integrity from His people. In Amos' day there were bribery, oppression, violence and robbery on every hand. These were the life-style of the people. And yet built into the covenant that God had made with His people was concern for the rights of all persons—the slaves, the foreigners, the widows, the poor.

When you and I think of justice, we think of blind justice in Roman terms—holding out the scales, trying to be absolutely fair and impartial. But justice in the Bible is open-eyed. It passionately seeks out wrong and tries to right it. It is dedicated to other people's needs and especially the needs of those less able to care for themselves.

The justice that Amos calls for is desperate to share with others what God has done for us. In contrast, Amos denounces some rich women who were called "cows of Bashan." Living in rich luxury, growing fat like well fed cows, they sit in the mountain of Samaria. And yet they oppress the poor and crush the needy and badger their husbands to earn more money so that they live it up in opulence. Unbridled selfishness! (Amos 4:1–3).

Not just strong sentiment but determined action is what God wants. Not just pious expressions but *right relationship*—that is what the God of justice and righteousness demands. The time is right for us to begin to catch up with the Bible.

Right relationship includes loyalty, obedience, and compassion. What Amos taught in the Old Testament James echoed in the New: "Religion that is pure and undefiled before God and the Father is this: to visit orphans and widows in their affliction, and to keep oneself unstained from the world" (Jas. 1:27).

How do you stand with the God of righteousness and justice? Well, you do not. You fall on your face and you ask forgiveness for your foolishness and sentimentality

—for your failure to worship God as God and to serve Him without reserve. He will forgive. He has more compassion for us than He asks from us toward others—and that is plenty.

Prayer: *Great God of righteousness and justice, write within our hearts your law of love and your concern for others that our lives may reflect your attitude toward them. As we rest secure in your sovereignty over history, may we be restless to share your compassion with men and women everywhere. Through Jesus Christ our Lord. Amen.*

4
Does It Cost Too Much to Be Nation No. 1?

Obadiah: God Speaks to a Nation Captured by Its Pride

Obadiah 1:1–4
The vision of Obadiah.
Thus says the Lord GOD concerning Edom:
We have heard tidings from the LORD,
*   and a messenger has been sent*
*   among the nations:*
"Rise up! let us rise against her for
*   battle!"*
Behold, I will make you small among the
*   nations,*
*   you shall be utterly despised.*
The pride of your heart has deceived
*   you,*
· you who live in the clefts of the
*   rock,*
*   whose dwelling is high,*
who say in your heart,
*   "Who will bring me down to the ground?"*
Though you soar aloft like the eagle,
*   though your nest is set among the stars,*
*   thence I will bring you down,*
*   says the LORD.*

Introduction to Obadiah

When Rebekah, the wife of Isaac, was about to give birth to twin sons, the Lord told her that two nations were in her womb, two brothers would be divided and the elder would serve the younger. The younger son was Jacob, through whom God gave the covenant, the promise to His people Israel. The elder was Esau, whose descendants became the Edomites, a nation usually antagonistic to Israel.

Obadiah, "the servant of the Lord," received a vision from God concerning Edom somewhere in the period between 570–450 B.C. This nation, south of the Dead Sea, had been judged by God for the pride and cruelty she demonstrated when Jerusalem was destroyed in 587 B.C. (vv. 1–14). The Edomites' judgment was an aspect of universal judgment (vv. 15,16). They had participated in the destruction of Jerusalem and would be subjugated with "no survivor" when God restored the "house of Jacob" and made Mount Esau the Lord's kingdom (vv. 17–21).

This short book is written in vigorous poetic style which addresses Edom directly in the words of God. The message is almost exclusively to the non-Israelite nation and is expressed in brilliant metaphors and an effective use of the repetition which is the mark of Hebrew poetry.

The corridors and cloakrooms at the United Nations are abuzz. Secretaries and pages range through the giant box of glass and steel seeking delegates and ambassadors. In a scurry the officials take their seats. The gallery fills in minutes. News reporters and photographers have pencils racing, tapes turning, cameras whirring.

What has put that grand assembly in such a dither? A statesman losing his temper? Maybe, but not likely. That has happened before. Ambassadors have blasted each other with such explosiveness that translation has hardly been necessary. Whole delegations have stomped out of the hall. A head of state has driven home his point with the heel of his boot.

Perhaps it is good news that has the United Nations General Assembly astir. Not necessarily. It has known its share of happy announcements from the Korean armistice, through the quieting of hostility in Nigeria, to the withdrawal of Pakistani troops from Bangladesh. Good news the United Nations enjoys. And it could do with more. But good news would not account for the stir I described in this imaginary scene.

What would? What would probably shock the United Nations most would be for a nation to stand before the solemn assembly and make a public apology. You can hear the speech now: "Mr. Secretary, ladies and gentlemen. I have been instructed by my government to tell you that we have made a serious mistake. We had no right to move our troops across the borders of our neighbors to invade their land. Furthermore, the stories of provocation were lies. Our neighbors have done nothing to provoke this invasion. We did it purely from greed and selfishness. The arguments that we brought to the Security Council on our behalf were fallacious, if not downright false. And to this august gathering, which has been justly angry at our action, my government wants to tender a sincere apology."

"Ridiculous!" you say. You are probably right for two reasons. First, international disputes are rarely that simple; and second, nations never seem to apologize.

National pride is not an easy idea to get hold of. There's a side to it that may be necessary and wholesome. Good government depends on people who care about their country, and national security hinges on enough pride to keep selfish and aggressive neighbors from encroaching on our terrain.

But national pride has a sick side as well. It may cause us to puff up our own importance in a way that hurts us and others. It may give us an excuse to trample the rights of other countries that we deem less important. It may nurture a smugness within us that makes us think we are self-sufficient, not dependent on God or man.

With new nations struggling for identity and recognition, with old nations slipping in power and prestige, national pride is a current problem. People of our generation have not done too well in dealing with it. Part of the reason for our failure is that we have tried to solve our national problems with our Bibles closed. We have some catching up to do. But it would not take us long if we opened the Bible to one of the shortest books, the message of the prophet Obadiah. You can read it through in five minutes or so.

Foolish National Pride

Obadiah is the only Old Testament prophet whose entire message is directed toward a foreign country. Edom was Judah's southern neighbor. More than that, Edom and Israel were related. The tribes of Israel, all 12 of them, descended from the sons of Jacob. The men of Edom were the offspring of Esau, Jacob's twin. So by geography and ancestry Judah, as we call the southern part of Palestine, and Edom had a lot in common. Yet conflict and warfare were a way of life with them. Border raids, disputes over water, ambush of caravans, and even whole-scale invasions were characteristic of their relationships.

Judah was not perfect. Not by any means! The books of Kings and the great prophets agree that the men of Judah were more often wrong than right in their national policies. But Edom had a severe problem that was almost chronic—a foolish national pride.

Obadiah gives two reasons for it: the Edomites were secure in their geography, and they were confident in their wisdom. Let's hear how the Lord describes this national pride and the reasons for it:

Behold, I will make you small
among the nations,
you shall be utterly despised.
The pride of your heart has deceived you,
you who live in the clefts of the rock.
whose dwelling is high,
who say in your heart,
"Who will bring me down to the ground?"
Though you soar aloft like the eagle,
though your nest is set among the stars,
thence I will bring you down, says
the LORD (Obad. 1:2–4).

The people of Edom lived in a rocky, mountainous land that offered them a large measure of protection. Even today one of the world's fascinating places is Petra, a city of Edom that was hewn out of red rock, accessible only through a narrow passageway walled in by sheer cliffs that defy climbing. A handful of men could hold off an army in that terrain. The Edomites took pride in their geography.

And their wisdom was legendary. In a culture where

men argued their points by telling parables and taught their children by using proverbs, the Edomites excelled. Riddles, word games, clever sayings, numerical puzzles were their stock in trade. They had answers for questions that had not yet been asked. For this reason God spoke directly to the pride they took in their wisdom:

Will I not on that day, says the Lord,
   destroy the wise men out of Edom,
and understanding out of Mount Esau? (Obad. 1:8).

Their pride of geography and cleverness made them highly vulnerable. "King of the mountain" we called the game when we were kids. One lad on top boasting of his strength, chiding the smaller, weaker fellows, egging them on by his arrogance. And more often than not they could topple him when they put their minds and backs to it. Then the next lad became king, and the boasting and toppling were repeated. So history has a way of dealing with proud nations.

Or watch how every team of athletes tries to outdo the champions. Upsets bring the greatest satisfaction. The prouder the champions, the more their opponents relish the defeat. A dangerous thing, foolish national pride.

Dangerous not only because of the animosity it creates but because of the harmful results it produces. A proud nation may readily become a cruel nation. Secure in its own purposes, ambitious for its own future, blinded to its own weaknesses, heedless of its neighbors' problems—it is ripe to hurt and be hurt.

Edom learned this painfully. Through Obadiah, God stingingly reminded Edom of his cruelty. Scene after scene is flashed on the screen like a newsreel at faster-than-normal speed.

For the violence done to your brother Jacob,
   shame shall cover you,
   and you shall be cut off for ever.
On the day that you stood aloof,
   on the day that strangers carried
      off his wealth,
and foreigners entered his gates
   and cast lots for Jerusalem,
   you were like one of them. . . .
You should not have entered the
      gate of my people
   in the day of his calamity;
you should not have gloated over
      his disaster
   in the day of his calamity;
you should not have looted his goods
   in the day of his calamity (Obad. 1:10,11,13).

Even worse, the proud cruelty of the Edomites led them to cut off those who were fleeing the invasion and to sell them as slaves. Edom was ripe for hurt. And ironically his hurt came from his friends, other desert peoples whom he trusted.

The mountain setting in which Edom took such pride became his trap, and the wisdom in which he placed such confidence turned to foolishness:

All your allies have deceived you,
   they have driven you to the border;
your confederates have prevailed
      against you;
   your trusted friends have set a trap
      under you—
   there is no understanding of it (Obad. 1:7).

Inescapable Divine Judgment

Behind this irony—where a fortress becomes a prison and wisdom is robbed of understanding—is the hand of God. Inescapable divine judgment is God's answer to foolish national pride.

This judgment is described so succinctly that we can miss its power. Indeed, we would rather pretend that it did not exist. But the prophet is too wise to let us deceive ourselves into complacency. Four key points he makes as he proclaims the threat of judgment.

God is thorough. "For the day of the LORD is near upon all the nations" (Obad. 1:15). In our foreign policy we tend to focus on one or two nations at a time. One month China has the headlines; another, Russia; still another, France or Italy. But in His greatness God can and will deal with all nations. None will be left out. Each must give account, whether it knows it or not.

God is fair. "As you have done, it shall be done to you, your deeds shall return on your own head" (Obad. 1:15). No more, no less than any nation deserves does God give. As Abraham warned at the beginning of Israel's history, the Judge of all the earth will do right.

God is merciful. "But in Mount Zion there shall be those that escape" (Obad. 1:17). A portion of God's people will be spared to carry on God's work, to make His name known, to celebrate His love and power. In the midst of judgment His mercy will shine. He is not through with the world. He may prune it back to get better fruit, but He will not utterly destroy it.

God is sovereign. On this note Obadiah ends His book. When God's judgment has purged the land of Edom of its pride (and all other lands as well), "Saviors shall go up to Mount Zion to rule Mount Esau; and the kingdom shall be the LORD'S" (Obad. 1:21). God's people will rule the once proud mountain of Edom, but the Lord will be the real ruler. This kingdom and all kingdoms belong to Him. This thought alone should squelch all foolish national pride.

An apology in the United Nations? Why not? Let Edom's terrifying example be a sign to all nations. Organize a tour of world leaders and take them to the land of Jordan. Walk through the once proud site of Edom and see its present desolation. Learn lessons from the lonely rubble. God is King. Let all nations acknowledge their mistakes, apologize for their crimes, repent of their sins. Let them bow before God who alone can forgive.

God himself has given the formula for national success. It is the way of *national humility*. "If my people who are called by my name humble themselves, and pray and seek my face, and turn from their wicked ways, then I will hear from heaven, and will forgive their sin and heal their land" (2 Chron. 7:14). This was God's promise to Israel, His special people. Whether God will work in exactly this way with *all* nations is hard to tell. But it certainly would be worth trying.

Prayer: Father, teach us the lessons that Edom learned; but if possible, do it at a lesser cost. Let neither our secure geography nor our accomplished wisdom be our crutch. You be our refuge, our strength, our hope. History knows that nations come and go. Your Word tells us that whoever does your will lasts forever. Let that be our story. For Jesus' sake. Amen.

5
We Can't Love Everyone, Can We?

Jonah: God Speaks to a Church Grown Cold

Jonah 3:1–5

Then the word of the LORD came to Jonah the second time, saying, "Arise, go to Nineveh, that great city, and proclaim to it the message that I tell you." So Jonah arose and went to Nineveh, according to the word of the LORD. Now Nineveh was an exceedingly great city, three days' journey in breadth. Jonah began to go into the city, going a day's journey. And he cried, "Yet forty days, and Nineveh shall be overthrown!" And the people of Nineveh believed God; they proclaimed a fast, and put on sackcloth, from the greatest of them to the least of them.

Introduction to Jonah

The book of Jonah is the biography (or autobiography) of Jonah, the son of Amittai, who lived in Israel, the northern kingdom. God called Jonah to go to Nineveh, on the Tigris River in Assyria, "and cry against it; for their wickedness has come up before me" (1:2).

Unlike other prophets who seemingly left their occupations and daily routines immediately to obey the call of God, Jonah fled in the opposite direction, away from Nineveh and (he thought) away from the presence of the Lord. His flight ended in the belly of the great fish (1:1–17). Jonah's prayer of complaint and thanksgiving prompted God to save him (2:1–10). However, God still had a message to be delivered to Nineveh and Jonah was the one to take it. So Jonah obeyed; he went to the city, delivered the message of judgment and the city repented (3:1–10). God heard the people, spared the city and angered Jonah. Chapter 4, verses 1–11 tell of the lessons of compassion that God taught Jonah.

The book gives very few personal details about Jonah's own life except the name of his father. If this Jonah is the prophet Jonah mentioned in 2 Kings 14:25, this narrative could have been written about 760 B.C. Many scholars, however, date the book much later.

Except for the prayer in chapter 2, the writing is prose narrative. The author recounts Jonah's story along with his conversations with God, and tells nothing about his preaching except that he warned, "Yet forty days, and Nineveh shall be overthrown!" (3:4). The message of the book is in the story: God is concerned for all people, even Israel's enemies, and He is anxious that His people understand this —so anxious that He will use His sovereignty over nature to get His point across.

Modern man is marked by a good bit of cockiness. He can tick off a long list of accomplishments older generations barely dreamed of. His progress has often cut him off from his past. His needs have changed, his problems are different, his opportunities loom large. What good will yesterday's approaches do in tackling tomorrow's issues?

This attitude often carries over in modern man's approach to the Bible. He thinks of it as part of the past, bound in buckram like the old books behind the glass doors in the museum. Beside the slick paperbacks and glossy magazines he reads to keep him abreast of modern styles, values, and culture, the Bible seems remote, tame, archaic. For ethical insights or guidance in personal problems he turns to the latest best sellers. Captains of industry, political leaders, psychological counselors, university professors, informed journalists, research scientists are the prophets of our society. And their writings are eagerly scoured by the curious and searching souls of our inquisitive generation.

If they want to review what people used to believe and what churches used to teach, they turn to the Bible, but only for historical purposes. Browsing through the Bible may even make them a bit nostalgic, as though they were leafing through the family album or remembering the old hairstyles in their high school yearbook. But to see the Bible as a textbook for handling modern issues—never!

Still, the question that we are asking in the title of this

book is not just a catchy gimmick. "Will We Ever Catch Up with the Bible?" is a legitimate question. There is much evidence in many areas that we will not. Family life, political responsibility, social maturity, religious duties, all could do with better clarification, higher motivation. When the full history of these last decades of our exciting century are written, there will be few high marks awarded for success in these areas. Could the problem be that we have insisted on looking in the wrong place for help?

No so-called modern prophet has rendered the old biblical prophets obsolete. Because they heard and spoke the Word of God they were ahead of their times then, and they still are now. Through them God addressed the problems that have plagued society and its various components in every age, problems that we are no nearer solving now than when the prophets first tackled them 2500 years ago and more.

As you have time you may want to look at the prophets, especially those who wrote shorter books, and see what they have to say to our day with its hurts and needs. To leaders abusing their power, to a world torn by calamity, God speaks through Micah and Joel. To a people yearning for Utopia, to a society devoid of responsibility, God speaks through Zephaniah and Malachi. To a church misguided in its priorities, to a nation captured by its pride, God speaks through Haggai and Obadiah. To an empire ensnared in its greed, to a world desperate about its future, God speaks through Nahum and Zechariah.

And *to a church grown cold* God speaks through Jonah. Most prophets convey God's Word by declaration. Jonah conveys it by illustration. Most prophets get their message across by recording their speeches. Jonah does this by telling his story.

We hardly need retell the story. Its basic outlines are known to almost everyone. A fugitive prophet saw his disobedience to God as the cause of a violent storm at sea and volunteered to sacrifice himself to quiet the storm. The ship's crew exhausted all other means of coping with the storm and as a last resort threw Jonah overboard. Not through with Jonah, "the LORD appointed a great fish to swallow up Jonah, and Jonah was in the belly of the fish three days and three nights" (Jon. 1:17). Hearing Jonah's plea, "the LORD spoke to the fish, and it vomited out Jonah upon the dry land" (Jon. 2:10).

Again God commanded Jonah to go to Nineveh, the proud capital of Assyria, and to preach God's message of judgment. This time Jonah obeyed. The citizens of Nineveh heard God's word, repented of their sins and were spared the promised judgment.

Here the story takes an unpredicted turn. Jonah was displeased at the Lord's grace toward Nineveh and told Him so. A second time God had to teach Jonah a lesson. This time He used not a fish but a plant, a plant that furnished pleasing shade for the disgruntled prophet. No sooner had Jonah begun to enjoy the shade than God sent a worm to attack and destroy the plant. Then a hot east wind and the Mesopotamian sun conspired to blister Jonah and make him ill.

We finish the story in the words of the text itself: and Jonah "asked that he might die, and said, 'It is better for me to die than to live.' But God said to Jonah, 'Do you do well to be angry for the plant?' And he said, 'I do well to be angry, angry enough to die.' And the LORD said,

'You pity the plant, for which you did not labor, nor did you make it grow, which came into being in a night, and perished in a night. And should not I pity Nineveh, that great city, in which there are more than a hundred and twenty thousand persons who do not know their right hand from their left, and also much cattle?" (Jon. 4:8–11).

That's the story, briefly told. But what about its meaning? The amount of actual preaching in it is just a few lines, the short summary of Jonah's sermon to the citizens of Nineveh. The message, then, has to be distilled from Jonah's experiences and especially from his conversation with God.

Jonah was a religious man. He knew the Word of the Lord when it came to him. Through his story God has spoken to religious people throughout the centuries. And through his story God still speaks to His church. In fact Jonah can be seen as an illustration of God's church, called to share God's message around the world. From Jonah's response, or lack of it, we can learn about our own. A church grown cold is what Jonah teaches us about. And Jonah's two responses to God's two calls give us the two main points of our message. Through Jonah God speaks to a church grown cold—a church grown cold in its obedience, a church grown cold in its compassion.

A Church Grown Cold in Its Obedience

God's first word to Jonah was brief and pointed: "Arise, go to Nineveh, that great city, and cry against it; for their wickedness has come up before me" (Jon. 1:2).

Jonah's reaction was almost as brief and pointed: "But

Jonah rose to flee to Tarshish from the presence of the LORD. He went down to Joppa and found a ship going to Tarshish; so he paid the fare, and went on board, to go with them to Tarshish, away from the presence of the LORD" (Jon. 1:3).

Whatever else we may say about Jonah's reaction, it was clearly an act of disobedience. God commanded him to go to one place and preach a certain message and Jonah headed in the opposite direction with anything but preaching on his mind. Nineveh lay to the east of Israel across the desert on the Tigris River in the northeastern part of the Mesopotamian Valley. Tarshish was probably a mining and metal refining area in Spain or Sardinia at the western end of the Mediterranean Sea. Jonah's intent was to get as far away as he could from the spot where God had spoken to him. Had he succeeded he would have been about 1000 miles from home and over 1500 miles from Nineveh.

In a sense Jonah's response is helpful to us. It shows us the humanity of the prophets. Almost always when the Word of the Lord came to the prophets, as it came to Jonah, they obeyed it. Hosea is a good example: "When the LORD first spoke through Hosea, the LORD said to Hosea, 'Go, take to yourself a wife of harlotry and have children of harlotry, for the land commits great harlotry by forsaking the LORD.' So he went and took Gomer the daughter of Diblaim, and she conceived and bore him a son" (Hos. 1:2–3). A succinct command followed by prompt obedience, that's the normal pattern.

But Jonah's deliberate disobedience is a useful mirror for us. In him we see ourselves, fearful of the call of God, uncertain about our mission, insecure in our gifts and talents, afraid of God's grace and its impact on others. Like Jonah, who paid his fare to Tarshish, we may pay almost any price to avoid paying the price that God asks of us as members of His Church, called to serve Him.

Jonah's willful disobedience was more than matched by the power of God's presence. Because the men of Israel met God in a special way in the Jerusalem Temple, they were sometimes tempted to put geographical boundaries on His presence. Their neighbors did this regularly, because they thought each deity had special power in his own realm but very little power in some other territory. Jonah must have thought that God's presence would thin out and weaken the farther he got from the Holy Land, as a radio signal tends to fade when we drive away from the transmitter. Jonah thought he could escape God's presence by fleeing.

But the great wind and the mighty tempest taught him otherwise. As members of Christ's Church we will do well to heed this lesson. Nothing that we do, nowhere that we go will free us from our responsibility to God. He has called us to His purposes, and we do best when we obey Him as faithfully as possible. No technological breakthrough, no contemporary philosophy is powerful enough to hide us from God's presence. Our modern neighbors trying to flee on foreign ships of politics, industry, or culture must learn this lesson. They should run hard to catch up with the Bible.

A Church Grown Cold in its Compassion

We learn a lesson from Jonah's disobedience but also from his obedience. "So Jonah arose and went to Nineveh, according to the word of the LORD" (Jon. 3:3).

The second time he obeyed God, and that's better than some of us do.

But God was asking for more than grim obedience. Jonah needed to learn about compassion. When the citizens of Nineveh, following the lead of their king, repented and were spared, Jonah was chagrined. Judgment he had preached, and judgment he wanted to happen. Nineveh's record of wickedness, ruthlessness, brutality, was common news in the Middle East. Jonah knew it well and wanted God to do something about it.

Furthermore, Jonah was probably jealous of his own reputation as a prophet. Jonah feared that he would be considered a false prophet when God refused to follow through with the judgment He had ordered Jonah to predict. Apparently this fear is what prompted Jonah to flee in the first place: "I pray thee, LORD, is not this what I said when I was yet in my country? That is why I made haste to flee to Tarshish; for I knew that thou art a gracious God and merciful, slow to anger, and abounding in steadfast love, and repentest of evil" (Jon. 4:2).

In a word, Jonah was more concerned for his standing as a prophet than he was for the salvation of people. Through him God speaks to a church grown cold in its compassion. We pray for the young people who are lost, and then are upset when they start coming to church with sandals and long hair. We ask God to renew His church, and then criticize the way He does it. We seek an outpouring of God's Spirit, and then tremble in fear of fanaticism.

God's command to us, as it was to Jonah, is not only to go but to care. Our reputations, our convenience, our comfort as God's people are secondary, secondary to our obedience and our compassion. God is well equipped to teach us these lessons painfully if we refuse to learn them readily. His sovereignty sent massive storm and giant fish, shady plant and gnawing worm to teach Jonah. He is no less sovereign and no less merciful now. Let's hope that we can learn our lessons at least as well as Jonah did. If we do we'll have begun to catch up with the Bible.

Prayer: Father, nudge us by your sovereign power till we go where you tell us, and warm us by your compassionate love till we care as you want us to. Let your forgiveness be more important than our pride. We want to learn, but like Jonah we need all the help we can get. Please give it to us in Jesus' name. Amen.

6
Does My Vote Mean Anything?

Micah: God Speaks to Leaders Abusing Their Power

Micah 3:9–12
Hear this, you heads of the house of Jacob
  and rulers of the house of Israel,
who abhor justice and pervert
  ·all equity,
who build Zion with blood
  and Jerusalem with wrong.
Its heads give judgment for a bribe,
  its priests teach for hire,
  its prophets divine for money;
yet they lean upon the LORD and say,
  "Is not the LORD in the midst of us?
  No evil shall come upon us."
Therefore because of you
  Zion shall be plowed as a field;
Jerusalem shall become a heap of ruins,
  and the mountain of the house a
    wooded height.

Introduction to Micah

Perhaps Micah is best known for his prophecy concerning Bethlehem as the birthplace of the Saviour (5:2).

Micah received the word of the Lord around 740–720 B.C. during the reign of three kings of Judah: Jotham, Ahaz and Hezekiah. Two other prophets, Isaiah and Hosea, were also foretelling the doom and destruction of Judah and Israel at about the same time.

Most of Micah's message is addressed to his fellow tribesmen in Judah and Jerusalem, though occasionally he mentions Samaria, capital of the northern kingdom. Micah pronounces scathing indictments of sin and paints dramatic pictures of God's judgment against Judah and Samaria because of the failure of their corrupt and oppressive leaders— prophets, priests, kings—to demonstrate righteousness and administer justice (1:1—3:12). He presents a clear summary of the requirements God had made of His people and how they had failed to meet them (6:1—7:7). But then Micah, in bright sketches, tells of the hope for Israel's future (4:1— 5:15) including the glories of the Davidic kingdom when God, in His love, will restore His kingdom because of His unique faithfulness and forgiveness (7:8–20).

In spite of the corruption of the leaders of Judah and Israel, God loves His people and will see to it that the plans for His kingdom will be carried out. Micah's name means "who is like the Lord," and Micah the prophet ends his written prophecy with a play on this definition of his name when he says, "Who is a God like thee, pardoning iniquity and passing over transgression for the remnant of his inheritance? He does not retain his anger for ever because he delights in steadfast love. . . ." (7:18).

The hats are in the ring. Election year merges with election year, and there are so many hats in the ring that it is hard to tell where the ring really is. Candidates from several parties and several wings of each party continually elbow their way to the front and volunteer their services.

The political air is thick with analyses and counter-analyses, promises and counter-promises. Each candidate appears confident that he or she has the prowess to solve the problems that the combined skill of previous office-holders has found overwhelming.

This drive for political power, from local alderman to president of the nation, is a curious one. The lure of leadership is there all right, with its pull of power, its promise of prestige, its opportunity to bring change. And for many, there is a sense of responsibility that leads them to seek office. They feel indebted to their community or country and want to help it fulfill its highest potential. They remember that all that evil people need do to gain power is for good people to do nothing.

But at the same time, the quest for political responsibility is a gamble of high risks. The odds that one will lose are enormous. Not merely that he will lose the election, but that, even if he wins, he will lose. Complacency is so strong among us, let alone evil, that wholesome change is hard to bring about. The social and economic problems we face are so huge that a successful government, whether local, state or national, is one that can stave off disaster at least until after the election.

And leaders who seem to be successful can lose another way. They win an election or gain appointment to high office, and their power begins to go to their heads. They enjoy making decisions that affect the lives of other persons. They surround themselves with aids and helpers who bow to their whims and rubber-stamp their ideas. With so many people telling them how smart they are, they begin to believe that they are always right. Subtly, insidiously, they take on larger-than-life proportions in their own minds. And because they are so great, they feel that they deserve extra favors and benefits. Almost without knowing it they are ensnared in a network of pride, greed, and even corruption that injures those who look to them for leadership, and does intolerable damage to the leaders themselves.

Whatever progress we modern human beings may have made in technology and political science, the deeper problems of governing and being governed remain the same. Voting machines have taken the place of ink-stamp and paper ballot, but they cannot help us choose leaders wise and good. Computers can predict who will win almost as soon as the polls are closed, but they cannot judge who should have won. Research techniques turn up files full of information about the status of our problems, but they do little to correct them. Public relations experts and mass media can make a political leader famous, but they cannot make him admirable.

Where should we look for help as we select leaders or exercise leadership? May I suggest the Bible? The Bible, you say? What does the Bible know about the complexities of modern government with its problems of controlling inflation, regulating taxation, implementing foreign policy, administering welfare, and conserving natural resources?

True, the Bible may not help us with technical answers to our political and economic puzzles but it will give us something more important. It lays the foundation for all leadership by showing where authority comes from and how it is to be used. It fits political and social leadership into the whole scheme of life, instructing leaders in their responsibilities and followers in their rights.

And it is particularly sensitive to the greatest problem that leaders ancient and modern have faced—the abuse of their powers. In this crucial area there is little evidence that we are catching up with the Bible. Our laws have helped, so have the traditional limits on the power of government expressed in our constitutions and bills of rights. But self-seeking and exploitation go on nonetheless.

Most of the prophets of Israel and Judah addressed parts of their messages to the leadership of their day. Nathan's sharp rebuke of David, and Elijah's running battle with Ahab and Jezebel are classical examples. Isaiah had stern words for Ahaz, and a century later Jeremiah used his tongue and pen against the last three kings of Judah: Jehoiakim, Jehoiachin, and Zedekiah.

It is Micah, however, who devotes almost all of his seven chapters to this subject. With a combination of sharp insight and hot indignation he lays the blame of Judah's sins at the doorstep of the men whose job it was to lead the people in paths of righteousness.

The Failure of the Old Leaders

Israel's leaders were almost like parents to the people. Theirs was a patriarchal form of society—the family heads made decisions for the whole clan. Respect for the elders and their wisdom was built into the bone and marrow of Israel. The king, especially, was revered as the chief, the spokesman, the father, the shepherd of the people. They leaned on his judgment; they followed his counsel; they trusted his values.

What the leaders were, the people became. Righteous kings who depended on God and walked in the ways He commanded in His law often brought revival. Under the influence of kings like David, Jehoshaphat, Hezekiah, Josiah, thousands of men and women turned from idols to serve the Lord who had brought their fathers out of Egypt and had entered into solemn covenant with them.

Not that Micah ignored the sins of the common people. They too were responsible to God and stood in danger of judgment. But it was the failure of the leaders that put Judah's life in jeopardy. Judah, remember, was the southern kingdom with its capital in Jerusalem. After Solomon's death the kingdom of Israel split in two with Judah in the south and Israel in the north—composed of ten tribes with their capital at Samaria.

The failure of the leaders—this is Micah's first great theme, and he pushes it hard:

> Hear this, you heads of the house of Jacob
>> and rulers of the house of Israel,
> who abhor justice
>> and pervert all equity,
> who build Zion with blood
>> and Jerusalem with wrong.
> Its heads give judgment for a bribe,
>> its priests teach for hire,
>> its prophets divine for money (Mic. 3:9–11).

"Heads, priests, prophets." With these words Micah points a finger of accusation at the royal family, with its

74

kings and princes, and at the spiritual leadership of the people—priests and prophets.

The ruling household is his primary target and he saves his sharpest arrows for them:

> Hear, you heads of Jacob
> and rulers of the house of Israel!
> Is it not for you to know justice?—
> You who hate the good and love the evil,
> who tear the skin from off my people,
> and their flesh from off their bones;
> who eat the flesh of my people,
> and flay their skin from off them,
> and break their bones in pieces,
> and chop them up like meat in a kettle,
> like flesh in a caldron (Mic. 3:1–3).

Think of it! Their greed was so great, their hunger for wealth and power so fierce that they were like cannibals feeding off their own people. The guardians of peace and justice had become agents of savagery and crime. No wonder the people were confused! Their defenders had become their attackers. Lawless, vicious men there will always be in our kind of world, but when the lawless, vicious men are the government, where do the people go for help? They must feel like a little child who flees from a bully into the arms of his father, only to have his father hold him while the bully beats him.

And the prophets, who should have been denouncing this political wickedness with its exploitation of poor and defenseless people, went around smiling and preaching "peace," as though nothing were wrong. They were not just wrongly optimistic; they were wickedly opportunistic. They adjusted the message according to the fee that they received for it:

Thus says the LORD concerning the prophets
　　who lead my people astray,
　who cry "Peace"
　　when they have something to eat,
　but declare war against him
　　who puts nothing into their mouths (Mic. 3:5).
The priests, too, had failed in their job. They taught
the law and instructed the people in God's ways only
when the price was right. Failure compounded—
crooked rulers, greedy prophets, lazy priests. Each area
of leadership that should have lifted the sights of the
people to God and His Law had become bogged down
in corruption.

The Promise of the New Leader

But God had another word to speak through Micah,
a word bright with meaning to us who look back to the
New Testament and its Good News. Not just the failure
of the old leaders but also the promise of the New Leader is God's message to Micah.

The New Leader follows an old pattern. From David's
town and David's family he comes, with strong ties to
the past and bright hopes for the future:

　　But you, O Bethlehem Ephrathah, . . .
　from you shall come forth for me
　　one who is to be ruler in Israel,
　whose origin is from of old,
　　from ancient days.
　And he shall stand and feed his
　　flock in the strength of the LORD, . . .
　And they shall dwell secure, for now
　　he shall be great
　　to the ends of the earth (Mic. 5:2,4).

And we know Whom Micah has in mind, David's son, David's Lord, born in David's city. A New Leader feeding, not fleecing, His people; making them secure, not anxious. He is "great to the ends of the earth," as thousands of you can attest. Any human leader who tries to do this is in for trouble right from the start. Only the divine Son of God can be the great leader of the world.

The New Leader breaks new ground. Micah's hope for the final solution of the leadership problem is not a return to the past but a tremendous future. A future fulfilled in worship:

> And peoples shall flow to it [the house of the Lord],
>> and many nations shall come, and say:
> "Come, let us go up to the mountain
>> of the LORD,
>> to the house of the God of Jacob;
> that he may teach us his ways
>> and we may walk in his paths" (Mic. 4:1,2).

A future blessed with peace:

> He shall judge between many peoples, . . .
> and they shall beat their swords into
>> plowshares,
>> and their spears into pruning hooks;
> nation shall not lift up sword against
>> nation,
>> neither shall they learn war any more (Mic. 4:3).

What leader can possibly fulfill these prophecies of true worship and lasting peace? Only Jesus Christ who has come and will come again.

To leaders tempted to abuse their power, the Bible says: Change your ways; God has a vested interest in good leadership; He has even sent his Son to show us how to be good leaders.

To followers skeptical of political promises, disillusioned by poor performance, the Bible says: Look beyond your human leaders to Jesus Christ, God's man governing in God's name; work for political change where possible; then bank finally on God, who Himself never changes but who can change everything and everyone else. Tested by this advice from the Bible it looks as though our modern age has some catching up to do.

Prayer: Our Father, your Word always does us good, especially when it deals with the problems we all face. Micah saw the New Leader beforehand and rejoiced that you were sending Him. We really know what He is like and our hearts are overwhelmed with joy. When so much leadership looks bad, thank you for Him. In His good name. Amen.

7
Don't We Have to Get Them Before They Get Us?

Nahum: God Speaks to an Empire Ensnared in Its Greed

Nahum 3:16–19
You increased your merchants
*   more than the stars of the heavens.*
* The locust spreads its wings and*
*   flies away.*
Your princes are like grasshoppers,
* your scribes like clouds of locusts*
settling on the fences
* in a day of cold—*
when the sun rises, they fly away;
* no one knows where they are.*
Your shepherds are asleep,
* O king of Assyria;*
* your nobles slumber.*
Your people are scattered on the
*   mountains*
* with none to gather them.*

Introduction to Nahum

About 620 B.C., Nahum, a native of Elkosh (a Galilean village), looked back at the glory and impregnability of Thebes, the city by the Nile, which was captured by the Assyrians around 663 B.C., and ahead to 612 B.C. when the Babylonians utterly destroyed the affluent and fortified capital of the Assyrian empire, Nineveh.

In his "oracle concerning Nineveh" Nahum begins by describing the sovereign Lord and His power to judge (1:1–15). He alternately speaks peace to Judah and doom to Assyria in acrostic poetry in which the successive verses of chapter 1 begin with the successive letters of the Hebrew alphabet. (Psalm 119 is the clearest Old Testament example of an acrostic.)

Then the prophet, speaking as though he were issuing commands to the defender of Nineveh, vividly describes the future siege of the great city. His words display a spirit of vindictiveness which shows how victims of Assyrian inhumanities longed for revenge on their oppressor (2:1—3:19).

The dynamic events of the last few years have changed the map of the world. I don't mean that new countries have been formed or that territorial boundaries have been shifted.

What I do mean is that new centers of power have come to the surface. Right after World War II the United States and Soviet Russia were the dominant world influences. What these super-powers did and said had striking impact on the rest of the world.

Recent years have brought dramatic change. A map

of world strategy no longer focuses on two major powers but on five. Alongside Russia and the U.S.A. stand the European Common Market countries—People's Republic of China, and Japan. The visits of our statesmen to China and Russia, together with their constant conversations with European and Japanese leaders have put a spotlight on the way the balance of power has been altered in our day.

New empires there may be. Or, more accurately, old empires may have come to power again. But this does not mean that our modern sages know all they should know about running an extensive and powerful government. Empires have been around for 4000 years or so, but we have not yet learned all their pitfalls.

The credit for forming the first real empire in history is usually given to King Sargon of Akkad, 2000 years before Christ. From his home base in southern Mesopotamia he moved northward conquering other city-states and binding them together in a network which he ruled. The clay tablet had as much to do with his success as did his military prowess. Rules and regulations could be scratched on the clay tablets and baked in to make them permanent. The tablets could be transported from the headquarters of the empire throughout its borders, making the king's will clear and providing firm guidance in affairs of state.

The ancient Mideast saw many empires come and go in the next 2000 years: Babylonia under Hammurabi, Egypt in the grand days of the Middle Kingdom, the Hittites about the time of Moses and later. King Solomon had an empire of sorts, and after him the Assyrians, the Babylonians again, the Persians, the Greeks under Alexander the Great, and the Romans all had their turn.

The rise and fall of these great empires can be charted in terms of military might, governmental efficiency, economic strength, and cultural achievements. But these gauges are not enough. To maintain their place of influence in the world, powerful nations today depend on trade agreements, economic alliances, cultural exchanges, adequate defense, treaties of nonaggression or mutual assistance, international diplomacy. But there is nothing new about any of this. Ancient empires did the same. And it was not enough.

The Bible knows a lot about empires. Some of the splendid kingdoms of history rose and fell during those adventurous centuries when men of God were hearing and writing His Word for our benefit. The prophet Nahum, for instance, devoted most of his book to an account of the collapse of the Assyrian Empire, which had reigned supreme in the Middle East for more than 250 years.

We have seen how the prophet Obadiah announced the fall of Edom, Judah's kin and neighbor. Edom's pride of geography and wisdom brought about her downfall. A tiny nation, aggressive and hostile, fell under divine judgment. But divine judgment is no respecter of nations. A small nation like Edom, a mighty empire like Assyria—they are judged alike by a jealous and demanding God. The empires of the modern world, empires in danger of being ensnared in their own greed, would do well to hear what the Bible said to Assyria 620 years before Christ.

A Reminder of Divine Sovereignty

Nahum wastes no time getting to his first point: the King of the universe is angry with His enemies. The

Assyrians and the men of Judah lived 600 miles apart. They spoke different languages and followed different customs. The citizens of Judah were God's special people. But He was still vitally and constantly interested in what the Assyrians did. The rivers, mountains, and deserts between Judah and Assyria were no barrier to Him. Nor was the Assyrian language foreign to Him. Assyrian culture He understood, understood well enough to be angry about what was going on.

His lordliness showed itself in wrath:

> The LORD is a jealous God and
>   avenging,
>   the LORD is avenging and wrathful;
>   the LORD takes vengeance on his
>   adversaries
>   and keeps wrath for his enemies (Nah. 1:2).

What would make a loving God, who had created the Assyrians along with all the other peoples, talk this way? What does it take for God to number a nation among His enemies?

God Himself gives two reasons—idolatry and inhumanity, worship of other gods and cruelty to people whom God made. God's language is strong:

> The LORD has given commandment
>   about you:
>   "No more shall your name be
>   perpetuated;
> from the house of your gods I will
>   cut off
>   the graven image and the molten
>   image.
> I will make your grave, for you are
>   vile" (Nah. 1:14).

Idolatry was their sin. The destruction of their idols was their judgment.

Powerful nations, mighty empires, are particularly prone to idolatry. In their pride and smugness they set up their own religious systems, religious systems which they then use to justify their greed and aggression. Their wars become holy wars because they have their god behind them prodding them on. Nazi Germany with its fierce sense of racial superiority, Japan with its fanatical commitment to its sun-god emperor in World War II, Communist China with its blind loyalty to chairman Mao—these are only a few recent examples of the mayhem that results when great peoples set up their own gods and follow them.

And the democratic nations of the western world have their own pitfalls. The will of the people is not necessarily the will of God. The American way of life with its materialism, apathy, and thirst for pleasure can itself become idolatrous.

Where idolatry is present, inhumanity is bound to follow. When a nation caricatures God, it devalues man. When it turns things into gods, it treats persons as things. Assyria, with her capital Nineveh, was no exception:

> Woe to the bloody city,
>   all full of lies and booty—
>   no end to the plunder!
> The crack of whip, and rumble of
>   wheel,
>   galloping horse and bounding
>   chariot!
> Horsemen charging,
>   flashing sword and glittering spear,

hosts of slain,
   heaps of corpses,
dead bodies without end—
   they stumble over the bodies!
And all for the countless harlotries
   of the harlot,
   graceful and of deadly charms,
who betrays nations with her
   harlotries,
   and people with her charms (Nah. 3:1–4).

Savage sin calls for savage judgment. This is Nahum's point. An empire built on cunning, greed and cruelty will collapse the same way. Like a prostitute she has lured other nations to consort with her and has left them diseased, robbed and ashamed. Her total influence has been destructive. Her power she has put to wicked purposes. Death and destruction are what she deserves.

Assyrian power was great. For over 200 years she sent her troops marching every spring. From the Persian mountains to the delta of the Nile, they marched. From the hills of Armenia to the coasts of the Mediterranean, they marched. And wherever they marched, they destroyed. No treasure was safe, no crop was left standing, no family was secure when the Assyrians passed through. They built their empire on greed and blood. Their power was great.

But God's power was greater. As King of the universe He had power to express His wrath, strength to carry out His judgment. When God comes to settle accounts with idolatrous and inhumane empires, the whole earth knows it:

The mountains quake before him,
   the hills melt;

the earth is laid waste before him,
  the world and all that dwell
    therein.
Who can stand before his
  indignation?
  Who can endure the heat of his anger?
His wrath is poured out like fire,
  and the rocks are broken asunder
    by him (Nah. 1:5,6).

Not that God revels in judgment. In fact He may put
it off as long as He can. But His patience with His
enemies runs out after a while, when they persist in their
waywardness:

The LORD is slow to anger and of
  great might,
  and the LORD will by no means
    clear the guilty (Nah. 1:3).

A Rehearsal of Divine Judgment

Assyria was guilty, and God refused to clear her.
Judgment became inevitable. Most of the book of
Nahum is given to a picture of this judgment. In the
dramatic language of a reporter on the spot Nahum
describes the judgment.

The sovereign God is at work, and the *judgment is
thorough:*

The river gates are opened,
  the palace is in dismay;
its mistress is stripped, she is
    carried off,
  her maidens lamenting,
moaning like doves,
  and beating their breasts.

Nineveh is like a pool
whose waters run away (Nah. 2:6–8).

The sovereign God is at work, and the *judgment is
terrible:*

Behold I am against you,
says the LORD of hosts,
and will lift up your skirts over
your face;
and I will let nations look on your
nakedness
and kingdoms on your shame.
I will throw filth at you
and treat you with contempt,
and make you a gazingstock (Nah. 3:5,6).

The sovereign God is at work, and the *judgment is
inescapable:*

Are you better than Thebes
that sat by the Nile,
with water around her,
her rampart a sea,
and water her wall? . . .
Yet she was carried away,
she went into captivity (Nah. 3:8–10).

The sovereign God is at work, and the *judgment is
deserved:*

There is no assuaging your hurt;
your wound is grievous.
All who hear the news of you
clap their hands over you.
For upon whom has not come
your unceasing evil? (Nah. 3:19).

There it is, a mighty empire reduced to a heap of
rubble. Three fierce nations—the Babylonians, the

Medes, the Scythians—came from south, east, and north and took the measure of Nineveh's might. The year was 612 B.C. and the proud capital has never been rebuilt.

Her epitaph could read: "Here lies the body of a greedy people, mistaken in its worship, perverted in its cruelty. It is gone but not missed. Its death brought peace as its life had brought terror."

Five great power centers in our decade, the political scientists tell us, nations full of might, of wealth, of promise. What will their epitaphs be? Can they do better than Nineveh? Only if they catch up with the Bible and what it says about the duty of nations: "Righteousness exalts a nation, but sin is a reproach to any people" (Prov. 14:34).

Prayer: Teach us, Holy Father, the lessons of good citizenship. May we do more than obey laws and pay taxes. May we show our fellow citizens and our government officials the way of life, the way of obedience to you. Through Jesus Christ our Lord and Lord of all nations, we pray. Amen.

8
Why Bother When It's All So Futile?

Habakkuk: God Speaks to a Society
Gripped by Frustration

Habakkuk 3:17–19
Though the fig tree do not blossom,
  nor fruit be on the vines,
the produce of the olive fail
  and the fields yield no food,
the flock be cut off from the fold
  and there be no herd in the stalls,
yet I will rejoice in the LORD,
  I will joy in the God of my salvation.
God, the Lord, is my strength;
  he makes my feet like hinds' feet,
  he makes me tread upon my high places.

Introduction to Habakkuk

About 600 B.C., in an impassioned argument between Habakkuk and his Lord, the prophet begs God to judge Judah for her intense corruption. God replies that He intends to allow the savage Babylonians who, under Nebuchadrezzar, had already defeated the Egyptians at Carchemish to deliver His judgment against Judah and her great capital, Jerusalem. Instead of rejoicing that God was not going to let evil go unpunished, Habakkuk chides God for choosing this solution. Then the prophet stations himself on a tower to see what God will say to him (1:1—2:5). One of God's great words was that the people who truly trust Him will be spared the judgment. This promise—"the just shall live by faith"—became the watchword of the Apostle Paul and Martin Luther.

Habakkuk pronounces woes on Babylon, the conqueror, on behalf of God's people, the victims (2:6–20). The prophecy ends with a hymn-like prayer in which Habakkuk describes the awesome majesty of God and proclaims his trust in Him despite the pending judgment (3:1–19).

The young man was in a frenzy, smashing shop windows, breaking car headlights, denting fenders. Bricks and stones flew in all directions as his wild anger played havoc with the neighborhood. The scene was the edge of the University of Wisconsin's campus. The time was the spring of 1970.

Two staff members of Intervarsity Christian Fellowship watched for a minute from a distance. As the young man paused to catch his breath in the midst of his fury, the two Christian men caught his attention: "Why are you doing this? What do you hope to accomplish by breaking everything in sight?"

"It's the war," he hollered. "It's that terrible invasion of Cambodia."

"But wait a minute," they answered. "Does it really help to solve the problem of war in Southeast Asia if you smash windows and damage cars in Madison, Wisconsin?"

"I suppose not," the young man admitted, "but I'm so frustrated I could break everything in sight."

There is not one among us with any humanity left in him who has not felt that way sometime in his life. We may not show our frustration in those weird and wild ways but we feel it just as keenly.

Frustrations we have by the bushel in every area of life. From threading a needle with a small eye to starting an old car on a winter morning; from cleaning up after small children to stretching a slim paycheck over a fat wad of overdue bills, we face continual frustration. Life reeks of it. But those are problems to look at another time.

The frustrations I am thinking of have to do with the helplessness we feel when we look at the out-of-joint course of history—the sharp frustration we feel about the great unsolved problems of our times. We are a society gripped by frustration.

What Makes Our Frustration So Great?

History has always been a frustrating process. Governments tend toward corruption. And the more powerful they become the more they use that power for corrupt purposes. It has always been that way. You would think that we would be so conditioned to inept and immoral government that we would shrug it off and go on our way doing the best we can. But instead we feel frustrated, trapped between our conviction that things should be different and our despair that we cannot change them.

Our frustrations are probably greater today than ever for a couple of reasons. First, *we are more sensitive to oppressing injustice and suffering.* Governments are no worse today than in the past. Business establishments and economic structures have always been manned by some dishonest people, and by those who cared and those who did not. When the Egyptian kings built the pyramids, thousands of slave laborers were used and undoubtedly hundreds of lives were sacrificed in the process of cutting and transporting and setting in place the massive blocks. And all just to provide a tomb for a king!

History knows some savage stories, from the death marches of the Assyrians who deported to foreign cities scores of thousands of their captives to the massacres of the Turks who killed more than a million Armenians early in our century. Violence and savagery have been with us a long time, but more and more we have grown to hate them.

The importance of the individual, the dignity of human life, the degrading effect of ruthlessness upon the spirits of those who give way to it—all these basic truths have sharpened our sensitivity to suffering. And at the same time our frustration has been increased. Part of this is due to the impact of Christianity. We have come to realize (or we ought to) that governments exist to benefit people not vice versa. And whenever our governments—local, state, national—fail to remember this, we find ourselves frustrated.

Second, *we know more than we once did about how bad the world is*. This too sharpens our frustrations. The mass media are largely responsible for this. The newspaper, the television, the radio bring to our homes daily reports from all over the globe. Wherever calamity strikes, wherever riot erupts, wherever corruption is uncovered, wherever crime is rampant, there photographers shoot pictures and reporters record interviews that are transmitted throughout the land. If a satellite can broadcast it, if a jet can speed the film clip to us, if tape recording can capture it on cassette, then we will see it and hear it within hours in our living room or kitchen.

Bombarded by this news, some people encapsulate themselves against it and watch it as though it were fiction, an interesting play but not really happening. Others do not bother to watch the news or read it at all. They find it too distasteful. But many read and watch in grim frustration, burdened by what they see and unable to do anything about it.

We know more about what goes on in the world than any generation in history. But our power has not grown with our knowledge. We have information about the facts of history that borders on the divine, but we have the same old human impotence when it comes to straightening out its crooked course. We have not yet caught up with the Bible.

What Can We Do About Our Frustration?

Our frustration ought to force us to look afresh at our faith. Is our Christian faith sharpening our frustration?

Are we frustrated because there are things we ought to be doing and are not? Is it partly a guilty conscience that tightens us up? If so, the answer is better discipleship, truer obedience. We may have failed to obey what we know we should do.

On the other hand, we may be frustrated by the sour turns of history because we have failed to apply what we know to be true. We may have trapped ourselves into looking at the world as though God were not in charge.

We can get good help on this problem from the Hebrew prophet Habakkuk. Six hundred years before Christ, he faced a problem similar to what we face today. History seemed out of hand, and God seemed not to care.

> O LORD, how long shall I cry for help,
>   and thou wilt not hear?
> Or cry to thee "Violence!"
>   and thou wilt not save? (Hab. 1:2).

Destruction, violence, strife, contention, injustice, lawlessness—these were the order of the day. And God did nothing about them. The people of Judah persisted in their wickedness despite Habakkuk's preaching, and God seemed to let them get away with it. But not for long.

His answer to Habakkuk's pleas for judgment comes in sharp and specific terms.

> For lo, I am rousing the Chaldeans,
>   that bitter and hasty nation,
> who march through the breadth of
>   the earth,
>   to seize habitations not their own (Hab.
>   1:6).

God goes on to describe the military efficiency of

these Chaldeans, or Babylonians as we call them:

> Their horses are swifter than leopards,
>> more fierce than the evening wolves;
> At kings they scoff ...
> They laugh at every fortress,
>> for they heap up earth and take it (Hab. 1:8,10).

Judgment is coming. The Babylonian armies will carry it out with dispatch. Habakkuk's frustration is not diminished but increased by God's answer. His reply to God is pointed:

> Thou who art of purer eyes than to
>> behold evil
>> and canst not look on wrong,
> why dost thou look on faithless men,
>> and art silent when the wicked
>>> swallows up
>> the man more righteous than he? (Hab. 1:13).

Judah is bad, but Babylonia is worse. Is it really justice for God to use a more wicked nation to judge a less wicked one? Absence of judgment was hard for Habakkuk to take, but this kind of judgment was even worse. The Babylonians were famous for ruthlessness. Now God was going to let them enhance their reputation at the expense of the Jews.

God's judgment was selective, not total. Those who depended on Him and were in turn dependable would live:

> Behold, he whose soul is not upright
>> in him shall fail,
> but the righteous shall live by his
>> faith (Hab. 2:4).

God's answer to Habakkuk's frustration came in three parts. First, *God would spare some.* His program would go on. He would see to it that His will was done despite the stubbornness of His people.

Next, He will also see to it that *the Babylonians themselves are judged* when they have completed their part in His program. They had no knowledge of His will. They mobilized their troops, planned their marches, ravaged the cities of their enemies to satisfy their own lust for wealth and power. God used their plans to carry out His. And they have to face judgment for their inhuman practices:

> Because you have plundered many
> nations,
> all the remnant of the peoples shall
> plunder you,
> for the blood of men and violence to
> the earth,
> to cities and all who dwell therein (Hab. 2:8).

The last part of God's answer to Habakkuk is as forceful as it is brief:

> But the LORD is in his holy temple;
> let all the earth keep silence before
> him (Hab. 2:20).

The Lord God is the ruler of history. He can be trusted even when history seems to be careening downhill, out of control. Our anxiety and frustration cannot solve the problem; His lordship will have to do it.

Habakkuk got God's point, especially after he was reminded of God's power and glory in one of the magnificent poems of Scripture (Hab. 3:1–15). The history of God's great deeds to His people flashes by the prophet in rapid scenes like a motion picture film speeded through the projector at faster-than-normal pace. The prophet is overwhelmed:

Though the fig tree do not blossom,
    nor fruit be on the vines,
the produce of the olive fail
    and the fields yield no food,
the flock be cut off from the fold
    and there be no herd in the stalls,
yet I will rejoice in the LORD,
I will joy in the God of my salvation
    (Hab. 3:17,18).

He began with frustration as we so often do. He ended with joy as we can too. What made the difference? He saw that God was Lord and trusted Him to do what was right.

"But this is a form of escapism, isn't it?" I can hear your question from here. To believe that God is Lord is involvement not escape. It means doing what we can where we are and leaving the rest to Him. For God is the Saviour of the world; we are not. He has sent His Son to make things right, and we can trust Him to do just that.

But He has also sent His Son to teach us to love our neighbor as ourselves. God loves the world, only He can do that. But our neighbors—those who come across our path, those whose lives touch ours, those who are in our circle of influence, those whose needs we have resources to meet—our neighbors are our responsibility.

When as modern men and women we begin to catch up with the Bible, we do not snap off the bad news; we do not take a pill to tranquilize ourselves in pseudo-happiness; we do not watch tragedy in a hypnotic stupor as though it were not happening. We believe in God. We have hope about history, because we know its final outcome. We have a perspective no news commentator can

97

give. God is Lord. He rules, and He calls us to use our time, energy, wealth, vote and influence to make His rule effective right now and right where we are.

Violence or apathy, anxiety or escapism; none of these is the answer to our frustration. Expectation for the future; service in the present, these are the answers. God's lordship crowds out frustration and puts hope and love in its place.

Prayer: Our Father, open our eyes to your larger plan for history. We have peered at our newspapers and squinted at our TV sets so long that we have tunnel vision. Broaden our perspectives to see that Jesus' lordship, His Kingdom, His coming are more real, more true than all the tragedy around us. And while we wait for Him to do His work, help us to do ours as part of His. In His hopeful name, we pray. Amen.

9
Whatever Happened to Our Grand Idealism?

Zephaniah: God Speaks to a People Yearning for Utopia

Zephaniah 3:17–20
The LORD, your God, is in your midst,
    a warrior who gives victory;
he will rejoice over you with gladness,
    he will renew you in his love;
he will exult over you with loud singing
    as on a day of festival.
"I will remove disaster from you,
    so that you will not bear reproach
        for it.
Behold, at that time I will deal
    with all your oppressors.
And I will save the lame
    and gather the outcast,
And I will change their shame into
        praise
    and renown in all the earth.
At that time I will bring you home,
    at the time when I gather you together;
yea, I will make you renowned and praised
    among all the peoples of the earth,
when I restore your fortunes
        before your eyes," says the LORD.

Introduction to Zephaniah

When, at the age of eight, Josiah came to the throne of Judah, the nation was steeped in wickedness brought on by Manasseh and Amon who reigned before Josiah and "did evil in the sight of the Lord." In a few years Josiah began to remedy some of the problems that the prophet Zephaniah decried.

About 625 B.C., before Josiah's major reforms got underway, Zephaniah had warned Judah and especially Jerusalem, with which he was intimately acquainted, that the "day of the Lord is at hand"; the day of wrath, distress and anguish would be upon Judah if her leaders and people did not repent (1:1—2:3). The neighboring nations of Moab and Ammon, and strong empires of Egypt and Assyria would not escape the judgment of God either (2:4-15).

Judah's salvation would not come from foreign alliances. Her only hope was in wholehearted repentance and humble trust in her God. Along with his declaration of woe to Jerusalem, Zephaniah promises hope beyond judgment (3:1-20). "On that day . . . the Lord your God . . . will renew you in his love . . . [He will] bring you home . . . [and] will make you renowned and praised among all the peoples of the earth."

Have you looked at a map of the world lately? No end to the changes. Dozens of new countries have been added since World War II, especially in Africa. Our geography textbooks have been thoroughly revised, and the maps of almost every continent redrawn.

Whole new color schemes have had to be designed. Where once the colors of England, France, Holland,

Belgium, Portugal, and Italy splotched the maps of Africa, South America, Southern Asia, and the Pacific Islands, now independent countries proudly bear their own colors. And the former colonial giants have shrunk to the modest size of their European boundaries.

As country after country gained its freedom, as territory after territory, mandate after mandate, was chopped into its traditional compartments by tribe or terrain, the same scene was repeated. Unbridled jubilation, ecstatic celebration. Independence days had the same look around the world: crowds jamming the streets and teeming in the squares, banners blazoning the bright colors of the fledgling flag, shouts of freedom and equality echoing through the capital. The language and style may vary, but the spirit is the same. Anthems and slogans, speeches and parades, banquets and festivals—these are the blankets in which newborn nations are wrapped.

The common denominator among them is high hope. Gone is the oppressive past when their lives were determined by others. Gone is their sense of futility and shame over the exploitation of their land and the rejection of their culture. Day has dawned with great expectations and deep yearnings—yearnings for utopia.

At its christening, each nation vows that the future will be different. The problems that plagued the past will be put down. Every person will be treated with dignity and every person will have enough.

But when the tumult and shouting die, when the debris of celebration is cleared from the streets, the tough job of converting slogan to action begins. And with it comes a return to realism. The dream of a better life tomorrow is often overshadowed by the struggle for survival today. Elbowing their way into the circle of powerful nations takes more muscle than they can muster. The heroes on whom they pinned their hopes expose their feet of clay. Yet the yearning for utopia goes on.

These feelings are not foreign to us Americans—the dream of utopia coupled with the reality of failure. Two hundred years ago we redrew the map of North America and turned colonies into states. We too had our independence day, and still do. We rejoice in our accomplishments and are heedful of our errors. We yearn for utopia and doubt that we will live to see it.

This tension is nothing new. Modern man did not invent this combination of bright vision and dark reality. The prophets of the Bible, with their rare blend of political insight and spiritual understanding, knew all about it. Six hundred years before Jesus came with His good news of God's love, a prophet named Zephaniah looked at his society and saw its shattered hopes.

The Emptiness of Our Idealism

If any nation had a bright beginning, it was ancient Israel. Her ancestry was unique. Abraham was her father, a magnificent man of courage and devotion. A man so singular in his devotion that he was called a friend of God. Israel's beginnings were miraculous—plagues that confounded the Egyptian king, a sea that divided, a desert that gave forth water, a land that awaited conquest.

And Israel had the Law, a constitution drafted by God Himself. The lives of the people were regulated by the commands of God. These commands protected the Israelites from the hurtful and foolish behavior of their neighbors. They were of all people most blessed. God was committed to them in a solemn covenant. They had His power for their protection, His wisdom for their guidance, His grace for their encouragement.

Even their capital city, Jerusalem, was a gift of God. He enabled King David to snatch it from the hands of the Jebusites, and He gave Solomon the wisdom and wealth to adorn its mountaintops with Temple and palace.

These marvelous beginnings seemed to promise Israel a brilliant destiny. In fact, God had made specific promises to Abraham and his sons that the men of Israel came to bank on: "And I will make of you a great nation, and I will bless you, and make your name great, so that you will be a blessing. I will bless those who bless you, and him who curses you I will curse; and by you all the families of the earth shall bless themselves" (Gen. 12:2, 3).

Israel's citizens can scarcely be faulted for their idealism. God had marked off for them a key role in His program for the world. Through them He was to make His name known. They were to be an object lesson to the world of true worship, true obedience. And at times they came close to achieving their ideal.

But as the centuries wore on, they forgot the responsibilities that went along with their privileges. They took God's care and grace for granted and lost sight of their mission and purpose as a nation. When this happened their idealism turned to hollow hope. Their great expectations of a bright future turned to empty wishful thinking.

Their leaders became corrupt, and their citizenry became complacent. This combination proved near fatal to the nation. The picture Zephaniah paints is a grim

one. A people that began with so much hope and promise was threatened with a fearful end. Their idealism had
come up empty, but they hardly knew it:

> Woe to her that is rebellious and defiled,
>> the oppressing city!
> She listens to no voice,
>> she accepts no correction.
> She does not trust in the LORD,
>> she does not draw near to her
>>> God (Zeph. 3:1,2).

This was Jerusalem, the holy city, that Zephaniah is
describing. The city where people should have worshiped God in truth, where they should have cared for
each other in love, had become utterly callous to the law
and will of God. At the heart of Israel's faith was the
command to hear: "Hear, O Israel: The Lord our God
is one Lord" (Deut. 6:4); yet now Jerusalem was listening to no voice. At the core of Israel's worship was the
invitation to come (Ps. 100:2,4):

> Come into his presence with singing!
> Enter his gates with thanksgiving,
>> and his courts with praise!
> Give thanks to him, bless his name!

Yet now Jerusalem refused to draw near to Him.

The leaders were to blame. Zephaniah minces no
words about this:

> Her officials within her
>> are roaring lions;
> her judges are evening wolves
>> that leave nothing till the morning.
> Her prophets are wanton,
>> faithless men;
> her priests profane what is sacred,

they do violence to the law (Zeph. 3:3,4).

No wonder Israel's idealism had become empty. Life itself had turned topsy-turvy. Every area of leadership was corrupt, bogged down in the very wrongs it was supposed to correct: judges were crooks; prophets were liars; priests were lawbreakers.

And all this in spite of God's loyalty to His covenant pledges:

> The LORD within her [Jerusalem] is righteous,
>> he does no wrong;
> every morning he shows forth his justice,
>> each dawn he does not fail;
>> but the unjust knows no shame (Zeph. 3:5).

Under this kind of wicked leadership Israel had compromised her uniqueness. She tried to live off her splendid past without being true to it. Idolatry thrived side by side with the worship of the Lord:

> I will cut off from this place the
>> remnant of Baal
>> and the name of the idolatrous priests;
> those who bow down on the roofs
>> to the host of the heavens;
> those who bow down and swear to
>> the LORD
>> and yet swear by Milcom (Zeph. 1:4,5).

The royal family led the way in this compromise. They became fascinated with the cultures and customs of their rich neighbors like Egypt and Assyria, and imported their corrupt and selfish ways:

> I will punish the officials and the
>> king's sons
>> and all who array themselves in
>>> foreign attire . . .

and those who fill their master's house
    with violence and fraud (Zeph. 1:8,9).

Corruption at the top and complacency underneath,
this was the pattern that destroyed Israel's idealism. The
people were blind to their plight. They were sick without
knowing it. Even worse, they did not think their condi-
tion made any difference to God. Zephaniah let them
know how wrong they were:

    At that time I will search Jerusalem
      with lamps,
     and I will punish the men
    who are thickening upon their lees,
      those who say in their hearts,
    "The LORD will not do good,
      nor will he do ill" (Zeph. 1:12).

The complacency of the people is compared to the
thickening of wine as it ferments. They don't do much
but sit and grow stodgy while the nation hurtles toward
judgment.

A stern warning, this. No nation can be carried to
success by its bright past or its sense of destiny. It needs
to be faithful to its calling along the way.

The Fullness of God's Salvation

God's answer to an idealism drained of hope by corruption and complacency is not to try to revive the
idealism. The leaky tire of human aspirations cannot be
pumped up with the hot air of economic suggestions or
political solutions. Philosophers and educators may
share their helpful theories with a disillusioned public,
but more is needed.

Salvation that is full is God's answer to an idealism
that has become empty. But this salvation may begin

strangely—with *a judgment that purges*. The more sorry the nation's plight, the more sweeping God's judgment needs to be:

"I will utterly sweep away everything
from the face of the earth," says
the LORD.
"I will sweep away man and beast;
I will sweep away the birds of the air
and the fish of the sea.
I will overthrow the wicked;
I will cut off mankind
from the face of the earth," says
the LORD (Zeph. 1:2,3).

Sounds like the flood in Noah's day, doesn't it? Judgment widespread and terrible. But how else does God deal with corruption and complacency? How else does He teach men that nations are to serve Him rather than their own interests?

Armament won't save them:

A day of wrath is that day,
a day of distress and anguish,
a day of ruin and devastation,
a day of darkness and gloom,
a day of clouds and thick darkness,
a day of trumpet blast and battle cry
against the fortified cities
and against the lofty battlements (Zeph. 1:15,16).

Wealth won't save them:

Neither their silver nor their gold
shall be able to deliver them
on the day of the wrath of the LORD
(Zeph. 1:18).

Armament and wealth won't save them. But God

Himself will. After He has sent the judgment that purges, He will offer *the grace that saves:*

> Then I will remove from your midst
>   your proudly exultant ones,
> and you shall no longer be haughty
>   in my holy mountain.
> For I will leave in the midst of you
>   a people humble and lowly.
> They shall seek refuge in the name
>   of the LORD (Zeph. 3:11,12).

The message that began with gloom and judgment ends with hope and praise:

> Rejoice and exult with all your heart,
>   O daughter of Jerusalem!
> The King of Israel, the LORD, is in
>   your midst;
>   you shall fear evil no more (Zeph. 3:14,15).

Not utopia but God's grace working among us, not idealism but His salvation, not our achievements but our repentance—this is the formula for a bright future. New nations, old nations—all nations God is calling to trust His name. Any other trust leads to bankruptcy.

Prayer: Here we are, Father, modern persons needing to learn ancient lessons. Your old book can bring us new wisdom. Teach us to read and learn. Show the family of nations the futility of their feuding, the insolence of their national pride. Be God to all nations on your terms. And start with us. For Jesus' sake. Amen.

10
How Can They Just Keep Asking for Money?

Haggai: God Speaks to a Church Misguided in Its Priorities

Haggai 1:2–5

"Thus says the LORD of hosts: This people say the time has not yet come to rebuild the house of the LORD." Then the word of the LORD came by Haggai the prophet, "Is it a time for you yourselves to dwell in your paneled houses, while this house lies in ruins? Now therefore thus says the LORD of hosts: Consider how you have fared."

Introduction to Haggai

Sixty-seven years before Haggai gave this precisely dated series of messages from the Lord, the city of Jerusalem had been besieged. The king's house and every great house of Jerusalem, as well as the house of the Lord, had been burned. What the Babylonians could not loot from the Temple they had destroyed. The walls around the city were broken down and the people still remaining in the city were carried into exile.

Now in 520 B.C. the exiles had returned to Jerusalem. In their desire to rebuild a nation they had set to work building new homes for themselves and restoring their economy—while the great Temple of Solomon lay in ruins.

The Lord, through Haggai, warned that He was displeased with the selfishness of the people who had put their own building projects ahead of His house (1:1–15).

Then the Lord sent a message to Zerubbabel the governor, and Joshua the priest (2:1–9). He promised that the glory of their Temple would outstrip the glory of Solomon's despite their modest circumstances as a puppet state controlled by Persia, which had succeeded Babylonia as the dominant middle eastern power (539 B.C.).

The next message from God was directed to the priests (2:10–19). It was a reminder that the fresh beginning symbolized in the Temple's new foundation would, in God's time, purge the people of sin and bring God's blessing.

The last message was a personal word to Zerubbabel. It promised him God's protection amid the turbulent time of Persian domination (2:20–23).

This prophecy of Haggai has a priestly emphasis that shows itself both in the preoccupation with the Temple and in the argument from Jewish ritual which underlies the third speech. In the description of the glories that are promised to

Show me your checkbook, and I'll tell you something about your faith. Checkbook? Faith? What do they have to do with each other? Why, come to my house and you'll see what I believe. The Bible on the coffee table, the shelves of religious books, the sign of the fish on the front door as a symbol of my Christian faith, the bumper sticker that says "Smile, God loves you." These are evidences of my Christian faith. But my checkbook?

I'll say it again: Show me your checkbook, and I'll tell you something about your faith. This was a lesson our family learned when my mother died. She had been a widow for three years and lived frugally on a modest salary from the church she served. When she died, my sister, Laura, who was in charge of mother's estate, went through her checkbook and was amazed to discover that mother was giving away nearly half of what she earned to Christian causes.

Particularly touching to my wife, Ruth, and me was a check stub dated March 1955. It contained the simple note in my mother's handwriting: "A thank-offering for Mary Ruth." We were in Scotland at the time our daughter Mary was born. Mother was concerned about the welfare of the new baby, because our first child had lived only a few weeks, too frail to survive in our kind of world. "A thank-offering for Mary Ruth" the check stub said. A grateful grandmother not only shared with her friends the good news of a baby born strong and well, she gave a gift to God. Her checkbook spoke volumes about her Christian faith.

This attitude toward money my mother learned from her lifelong study of the Bible. Though it's hardly a textbook on bookkeeping or economic theory, the Bible is the most important book on money that we possess. It tells us where it comes from, what we should and should not do with it, and why we have it.

How to use our wealth is among the most hotly debated issues we face. We will do well to get help from the Bible, especially from the prophet Haggai. Haggai's entire message, granted it's a short one, has to do with wealth—where we get it and how we use it. He reminds us that how we use wealth is a clear-cut indicator of what we think is important. Nothing announces our priorities more sharply than the way we open our wallets and checkbooks.

You have heard of the man who found himself in deep financial distress, job gone, savings exhausted. "We've moved out of our house into a tent," he told a friend. "My son has had to leave college; my wife has cancelled her medical treatments; my daughter is walking four miles to high school to save bus fare. If the situation gets any worse, I'll have to sell my Cadillac!"

Priorities—we can all act misguidedly at times. Even the church, God's people, who should be salt and light to the world, can confuse her priorities and put second things first.

This is just what had happened in Haggai's day. The men and women of Judah had straggled back to their homes after years of captivity in Babylonia, where they or their parents had been deported by Nebuchadrezzar. At the time that Haggai's message begins, they had been back in the land 16 years or so. All their energies had been consumed with the task of rebuilding their homes, reestablishing their businesses, restoring their farmlands, orchards and vineyards. Yet, despite all their efforts, they had not really prospered.

> Now, therefore, thus says the Lord of hosts:
> Consider how you have fared.
> You have sown much, and harvested little;
> you eat, but you never have enough;
> you drink, but you never have your fill;
> you clothe yourselves, but no one is warm;
> and he who earns wages earns wages to put
> them into a bag with holes (Hag. 1:5,6).

Against this frustrating experience of backbreaking toil and empty larders, Haggai utters the Lord's commands—commands that have special meaning to a church misguided in its priorities. First, *put God's work first*. Second, *believe that God's work is greater than it looks*, Third, *don't expect immediate returns*.

Put God's Work First

In their feverish efforts to get life going again after decades of captivity, the Jews had forgotten one thing—the house of the Lord. They had made a halfhearted start at rebuilding when they first came back, but they ran into some opposition from the Samaritans who had the run of the land while the Jews had been in exile. Immediately they quit. And the Temple foundations lay bare for the next 16 years, while the people tried to dig themselves out of their own problems. Then God spoke:

> "Thus says the LORD of hosts:
> This people say the time has not yet come
> to rebuild the house of the LORD."

Then the word of the LORD came by Haggai
    the prophet,
"Is it a time for you yourselves to
    dwell in your paneled houses,
      while this house lies in ruins?" (Hag. 1:2–4).

The magnificent Temple, the showpiece of Jerusalem, dreamed of by David and built by Solomon 400 years before, had been leveled by the battering siege and the blazing fires of Nebuchadnezzar's army.

Its stark ruins lay in marked contrast to the paneled houses in which the more affluent Jews lived. Haggai mentions the paneling to show that the houses were more than shelters from the elements. Typical houses in Judah were of rough-hewn stone from the rocky terrain of the countryside, or they were of clay bricks, packed in a mold and baked in the sun. Wood for paneling had to be brought down from the hill country in the north or from Lebanon where the famous cedars grew. Paneled houses spoke of comfort and elegance, while the Temple lay untended.

Go up to the hills and bring wood
    and build the house,
    that I may take pleasure in it
      and that I may appear in my glory,
    says the LORD (Hag. 1:8).

Coupled with this command is God's explanation of the lack of prosperity the people endured despite all their labors:

You have looked for much, and,
    lo, it came to little; and
when you brought it home,
    I blew it away.
Why? says the LORD of hosts.

Because of my house that lies in
  ruins,
while you busy yourselves each with
  his own house.
Therefore, the heavens above you have
  withheld the dew,
and the earth has withheld its produce.
And I have called for a drought upon the
  land of the hills, upon the grain,
the new wine, the oil, upon what the ground
  brings forth,
upon men and cattle, and upon all their
  labors (Hag. 1:9–11).

Put God's work first if you expect God's blessing. That's Haggai's first lesson. If someone were to look over your shoulder as you write your monthly checks, what would he find out about your priorities? House payments have to be made; we don't want to face eviction or foreclosure. Utilities must be paid; you can't do without light, heat, water, telephone. Hold out cash for food; need a little more now with prices going up. Insurance is due and so is the car payment. And then those credit card bills: gasoline stations and department stores have to have their cut of our income. Item after item we check off, and hope that month-end finds us with a small surplus for the Lord's work. Put God's work first, Haggai says, and you'll have more of what you need to take care of everything else.

Believe That God's Work Is Greater Than It Looks

Haggai's preaching got results. The people acted immediately. John Knox, the leader of the Scottish reformation, once preached a sermon against idolatry in the city of Perth. He had scarcely pronounced the benediction before his hearers rushed out on the streets and smashed all the statuary within several miles of the church. Immediate results!

And so with the preaching of Haggai. The leaders and the people "obeyed the voice of the LORD their God, and the words of Haggai the prophet, as the LORD their God had sent him; and the people feared before the LORD" (Hag. 1:12). Twenty-four days later they gathered to work on the Temple, and they had probably done a lot of planning and preparation in the meantime.

After they had been at it a month, Haggai spoke again to give them encouragement in their building. They needed encouragement for two reasons: They had heard reports of Solomon's splendid Temple, with its gold fixtures and cedar paneling; they had seen the elaborate temples and palaces of Babylonia during their days in captivity. They knew they were poor and could not compete either with their own past glory or the splendor of their neighbors. This discouraged them from the beginning.

God's Word spoke to their need:

> "Yet now take courage, O Zerubbabel
> [he was the governor, their highest-
> ranking political official under
> the Persian regime] . . .
> take courage, O Joshua [he was the high
> priest, the highest-ranking religious
> official] . . .
> take courage, all you people of the land, says
> the LORD;
> work, for I am with you, says the LORD
> of hosts,

according to the promise that I made with you
     when you came out of Egypt.
My Spirit abides among you; fear not"
     (Hag. 2:4,5).

Then God lifted their sights away from the meager
beginning to a day when the nations would bring their
treasures to His house. With great reassurance He
brought His promise to its climax.

The latter splendor of this house
     shall be greater than the former . . .
and in this place I will give prosperity,
     says the LORD of hosts (Hag. 2:9).

When you remember that it was in this house, rebuilt
by Herod, that Jesus taught and ministered, you can see
how literally Haggai's prophecy came to pass. What
greater glory could any Temple have than to provide a
setting for the Son of God to do His work?

We get confused in our priorities not only by putting
our own needs first, but also by gauging God's work in
human terms. Civic projects are impressive and presti-
gious. Public libraries render noble service. Boy Scouts
and YMCA programs seem to be reaching thousands.
Sometimes the church suffers by comparison. Why
should I give to it? What good will it do me to work for
Christian causes that often totter on the brink of failure?

Or some of you are in churches that once had great
crowds, teeming Sunday Schools, vital evangelistic programs. The people have moved away. A corporal's
guard remains, faithful but disheartened. Haggai's word
is good: believe that God's work is greater than it looks.
His presence that makes the difference. Don't judge His
mission by secular standards. "My Spirit abides among
you; fear not." And keep working and giving.

Don't Expect Immediate Returns

Haggai's third word to a church misguided in its priorities came three months after the rebuilding began. Evidently the people began to wonder why God had not yet kept His promise to bless them. They had tried to obey Him for 90 days, yet they were still living in poverty and depression. Using illustrations drawn from Jewish law, God taught them that evil is more contagious than good, that a little sin corrupts but a little holiness does not purify.

In other words, God was putting their obedience to the test. Were they really serious about their devotion? Would they stick with it? For three long months he tried them, and then, as they sighed with relief, He promised to bless.

Is the seed yet in the barn?
Do the vine, the fig tree, the pomegranate,
and the olive tree still yield nothing?
From this day on I will bless you (Hag. 2:19).

Don't expect immediate return. God is not a pump that we prime a little in the morning with our good works so that He will spill His blessing on us the rest of the day. He reserves the right to bless us if and when He is ready. Our task is to be faithful; the rest is up to Him.

We have not yet caught up with the Bible in sorting our priorities. The Bible is not only the book that speaks of God, it is the book that speaks of mammon. It warns against the love of money, the wrong use of money, the distracting influence of money. In a society consumed with talk of gross national product, guaranteed annual income, minimum wage, higher stock dividends, capital gains taxes, we need to catch up with the Bible to see what money is all about.

Haggai's plea was for a Temple. Jesus taught us that His body, the people of God, the church, is the temple of God in our day. We give and work not so much to build buildings as to lead people to sounder worship, clearer knowledge, richer service—worship, knowledge and service of the true and living God who came to us in Jesus Christ.

Charles Fuller's father taught him spiritual priorities when he was just a boy. He had to pay his tithe in gophers' tails. Well, not exactly in gophers' tails but in dimes earned in exchange for the gophers' tails trapped on the orange ranch near Redlands, California. To the Methodist church he took them, one dime for every ten he earned. Whether gopher tails, cash, stocks, bonds, real estate or crops—God wants His share first. Honoring Him takes priority over everything else.

Prayer: Father, we know that how we give says something about whom we serve. It is you—not mammon, not money, not goods—that we really trust. Without you nothing else matters. With you everything will be all right. Help us to learn to give you what costs because you have given us what we could not ever pay for—your love and forgiveness. In Jesus' name. Amen.

11
But What If They Push the Button?

Zechariah: God Speaks to a World Desperate About Its Future

Zechariah 12:10; 13:1; 14;8,9

And I will pour out on the house of David and the inhabitants of Jerusalem a spirit of compassion and supplication, so that, when they look on him whom they have pierced, they shall mourn for him, as one mourns for an only child, and weep bitterly over him, as one weeps over a first-born.

On that day there shall be a fountain opened for the house of David and the inhabitants of Jerusalem to cleanse them from sin and uncleanness.

On that day living waters shall flow out from Jerusalem, half of them to the eastern sea and half of them to the western sea; it shall continue in summer as in winter.

And the LORD will become king over all the earth; on that day the LORD will be one and his name one.

Introduction to Zechariah

God disclosed His purposes to the priest and prophet Zechariah through eight dramatic visions which showed His sovereignty and glory (1:1—6:8). The purpose of Zechariah's messages, like Haggai's, was to rally the people to rebuild the Temple and reaffirm their hope in God after the devastating decades of captivity in Babylon.

In chapter 5, verses 9–15, God gives Zechariah a description of Joshua the anointed priest in terms that point to the Messiah. Chapters 7 and 8 foretell that, as the Lord prospers His people, fasting will give way to feasting.

While the ministry and messages recorded in chapters 1—8 are contemporary with the prophet Haggai (520 B.C.), chapters 9—14 have provoked much scholarly debate concerning their date. In these chapters Zechariah foretells more about our Saviour than any other "minor" prophet. His prophecies are of the Messiah's first and second comings and His worldwide impact.

Chapter 9 announces judgment on Israel's neighbors as the great King comes to enforce peace. Chapters 10 and 11 describe the Good Shepherd who replaces the false leaders, yet is in turn rejected by His flock.

Chapter 12 pictures Jerusalem's victory over her enemies and her remorse as she looks on Him whom she had pierced.

Then in chapter 13 Zechariah foretells the cleansing of Jerusalem from sin and uncleanness and the blessings and judgments of God's coming Kingdom.

My friend knows the campus scene intimately. He lives in Berkeley and meets scores, if not hundreds, of students every week. He used to be a university professor and has the knack of reading the mood of the student generation. His travels take him to dozens of campuses every year.

He was a good man for me to put my question to. "What's doing on the campuses these days? What's the prevailing attitude?"

His answer came immediately and in one word: "Despair." He went on to indicate what he meant. "Not that we're on the verge of mass suicide, or that students find no enjoyment in life. What I mean by *despair* is that there is no true hope, nothing to look forward to that really matters."

Our despair is fed by what we hear about tomorrow. How long since you heard any optimistic prediction about the future? The modern prophets specialize in gloom.

Over-population! The prophets of gloom picture teeming cities, rapidly spreading so they touch each other and form great urban masses from San Diego to San Francisco, from Washington to Boston, from Philadelphia to Chicago. Six billion people are due to jam our spinning space ship within 25 years. And after that, matters only get worse.

And the danger of global warfare! Every time a conflict between two nations smolders and sparks we wonder what it will ignite. We feel about as safe as the driver of a gasoline truck caught in a forest fire. Behind every limited war stand major powers choosing sides. The results are scary. One misstep, one message misunderstood, one button wrongly pushed, and boom! That's it! That's why the struggles between India and Pakistan, between Israel and Egypt, between Lebanese Christians and Muslims, are so terrifying. In and of themselves they are awful—consuming priceless resources, destroying thousands of lives, embittering millions of minds, squandering the strength of noble nations. But what is truly frightening is the horrible potential of worldwide war. Think of it. All the world's technological skills would be directed to one end—mass murder of men called enemies.

Add to these fearful prospects the possibility of a world irreversibly polluted, and the hopelessness mounts. Rivers whose waters carry cancer, air that blackens the lungs of all who breathe it, land so loaded with junk or coated with chemicals that it won't sustain life—these are the telltale symptoms of the abuse of our environment, the only environment we have.

Small wonder that despair is almost a way of life with us. Any one of these prospects is grim enough—overpopulation, global destruction, planetary pollution. It's as though our world had run amuck, speeding wildly toward some bitter tomorrow.

Obviously we must do what we can, controlling population, finding new sources of food, pursuing peace, protecting and purifying our environment.

But our final hope can never hinge on man. Supervising the long-range plans for our globe is the One who made it. His great day is yet to come. Modern man needs to know this. Whether sluggish with apathy or scurrying in panic, modern man needs to know this. Desperate about his future, he needs to hear God speak.

And God has spoken, spoken through the prophet Zechariah, to a world desperate about its future. Twenty-five hundred years have come and gone since

Zechariah encouraged the weary men of Judah with his words of hope. They had been through long years of captivity. Their strength was sapped; their zest for life had ebbed; their hope of future glory was dimmed. Then Zechariah lifted their sights and buoyed their spirits with talk about the future, a future in which Israel would be truly converted, a future in which Jerusalem would be thoroughly cleansed, a future in which a new King would personally come to reign.

The Conversion of Israel

The prophets often sparked the hopes of their countrymen by promising a day when their enemies would be put down and the borders of Israel extended. And Zechariah also talks about this. But he connects it with a time when the men of Israel will go into deep mourning. This seems like a strange combination—high victory and deep mourning. Yet the prophets are never narrow nationalists. If Israel wins, it is not merely because she is Israel but because God is with her, or more accurately, she is with Him.

What Zechariah sees is a time when God will pour out on His people a gift of grace that enables them to repent and turn to Him whom they have rejected. Listen to God's own words:

> And I will pour out on the house of David and
>   the inhabitants of Jerusalem a spirit of
> compassion and supplication, so that, when they
>   look on him whom they have pierced, they
> shall mourn for him, as one mourns for
>   an only child, and weep bitterly over him,
> as one weeps over a first-born (Zech. 12:10).

Here the *holiness of God is at work.* Even His chosen

people need to be converted. He is no respecter of persons or races. He does not play favorites. He makes no excuses, even for the people who are bound in covenant to Him. They have sinned. They must repent.

The specific sin that Zechariah mentions is described in the words "when they look upon him whom they have pierced." What else can this mean than the crucifixion of Jesus? And not just the cruel act of pinning Him to the cross but the entire rejection of Him as Son of God and Messiah. Of this sin the people of Israel must repent. The holiness of God demands it. Jesus "came to his own home, and his own people received him not" (John 1:11). What an insult to the Son of God and the Father who sent Him.

But here the *mercy of God is at work*. The day is coming when God Himself will lead the people of Israel to see that what they did to Jesus in refusing to worship Him was wrong. They will mourn over their sins, and the holy, merciful God will forgive. And in His forgiveness lies the true hope for a world desperate about its future.

Change there must be. Change there will be—*the* change, change in attitude toward Jesus Christ. This is the ultimate change, the change from rejection of Jesus as God's man for the world to acceptance of Him. Zechariah says this will happen. And so does the Apostle Paul, whose own life had already experienced this change. Paul teaches his friends at Rome that when God has completed His work among the Gentiles He will turn again to the people of Israel and bring them to Himself: "And so all Israel will be saved; as it is written, 'The Deliverer will come from Zion, he will banish ungodliness from Jacob; and this will be my covenant with

126

them when I take away their sins' " (Rom. 11:26,27, quoting from Isaiah and Jeremiah).

The Cleansing of Jerusalem

Israel will be converted and Jerusalem will be cleansed—this is Zechariah's promise. The chosen people need to repent, and the holy city needs to be purified. Again the righteous God is making His will known:

> On that day there shall be a fountain opened
> for the house of David and the inhabitants
> of Jerusalem to cleanse them from sin
> and uncleanness (Zech. 13:1).

This is a graphic picture. Jerusalem is so defiled that the normal water supply is not sufficient to give her the scrubbing she needs. Water is a scarce commodity in the Bible lands, especially around Jerusalem. Hezekiah's workmen once dug a huge tunnel to bring water in. But now a new fountain is to be opened; without it the city cannot be cleansed.

Two questions pop up immediately. What had polluted the city? And what sort of fountain will it take to cleanse it? The first question Zechariah himself answers:

> And on that day, says the LORD of hosts,
> I will cut off the names of the idols from
> the land,
> so that they shall be remembered no more;
> and also I will remove from the land the
> prophets and the unclean spirit (Zech. 13:2).

Idolatry and false prophecy Zechariah mentions, putting his finger on the reasons for Jerusalem's corruption. Worship of false gods and heeding of incorrect information—this was her double sin.

127

Ironic these sins are. The city at whose center stood the Temple of the one true God had become a nest of idols. The city where the Word of God was to be heard most clearly had become a den of false prophets. Jerusalem needed cleansing.

But what about the fountain? Since it is sin that needs to be washed away, water will not do the job. Sin is like grease. Water cannot touch it: "Without the shedding of blood there is no forgiveness of sins" (Heb. 9:22). Not that blood is a solvent in a literal sense. But sin requires penalty, and the penalty for a sin like idolatry is the giving up of life. Idolatry is a capital sin that deserves capital punishment.

In His mercy God accepted the sacrifice of animals as a substitute for man. But in the long run something more was needed. Sin was too great, rebellion against God was too persistent, disobedience of God was too insulting to be compensated for by animals. A cleansing fountain had to be opened for Jerusalem and the world. So God sent His Son to bear our sins in His own body on the cross. The blood that dropped from His head, His hands, His side, His feet became the fountain that Zechariah foretold. Remember the words of the old hymn by William Cowper,

> There is a fountain filled with blood
> Drawn from Immanuel's veins,
> And sinners plunged beneath that flood,
> Lose all their guilty stains.

That's what Jerusalem needed. That's what God has done.

The Coming of the King

A world desperate about its future is a world that is

realistic. The future *is* dark, shadowed with uncertainty, gloomy with bad prospects. Like a letter edged in black, it holds little promise of bringing good news.

What contributes to the darkness is man's deep suspicions of his own ability to bring light. Left to us the future will remain dark. We are the ones who need to change. And we cannot change ourselves. Far from bringing rays of light, we add to the gloom.

But new life is coming. That is Zechariah's hope:

> On that day living waters shall flow out
> from Jerusalem, half of them to the eastern
> sea and half of them to the western sea;
> it shall continue in summer as in winter.
> And the LORD will become king over all the
> earth; on that day the LORD will be one and
> his name one (Zech. 14:8,9).

The desert will blossom, the seasonal drought will be ended, the water supply will be lavish, life will begin to flourish—and all because the King is coming.

The King Zechariah has mentioned before:

> Lo, your king comes to you;
> triumphant and victorious is he,
> humble and riding on an ass,
> on a colt the foal of an ass (Zech. 9:9).

This is Christ's first coming, and especially His majestic ride into Jerusalem on Palm Sunday. But a greater kingship is yet to come, when Jesus' lordship is recognized worldwide.

Then it will be that the people of Israel will turn to Him whom they pierced. Then it will be that the city of Jerusalem will be purged of idolatry and false prophecy. Then it will be that the nations of the world will bow before the one God, the Lord of life. He and He alone can bind peoples together and put down the hostilities, prejudices, anxieties that keep them apart.

Only God has the right combination of power and goodness to bring peace and good will. Weak reformers may have goodness without power; mighty dictators usually have power without goodness. Only the coming King—Jesus Christ, Son of God—has both.

I can hear two questions as you reflect on what Zechariah has been saying. What does all this have to do with me? The talk is about Israel and Jerusalem. I live in Calgary or Manila or Panama or Michigan. I'm a Gentile, not a Jew. Right you are! But the same need and the same possibilities exist. How have you treated Jesus? In a way you helped to crucify Him, and so did I. We pierced Him with our sin, our rejection, our insults. We need to turn to Him, and we can.

Idolatry and false prophecy are our problems too. That's why we are in despair. We worship false gods and obey false teachings. Cleansing is what we need.

"I can see that," you say, "but do we have to wait for the Second Coming?" Not at all. We need to learn lessons from some of Jesus' followers as we face the despair on our campuses, the despair in our offices, shops, kitchens.

Thomas looked at Jesus' pierced side and wounded hands and said "My Lord and my God!" (John 20:28). Peter, knowing that he had to be washed to belong to Jesus, said to the Lord who was about to wash his feet, "Lord, not my feet only but also my hands and my head!" (John 13:9). Nathaniel, whose guileless heart Jesus read, exclaimed: "Rabbi, you are the Son of God! You are the King of Israel!" (John 1:49). Conversion, cleansing, kingship begin not when Jesus comes, but now, when you in faith come to Him as King.

Prayer: Lord, you have shown us that modern man can have hope if he looks in the right place and to the right Person. Teach us that the right place is your Word and the right Person is our Lord. Build our hopes on nothing less than Jesus' blood and righteousness. In His trustworthy name we pray. Amen.

12
Me? Rob God?

**Malachi: God Speaks to a Society
Devoid of Responsibility**

Malachi 3:6–10
*For I the LORD do not change;
therefore you, O sons of Jacob, are not
consumed. From the days of your
fathers you have turned aside from my
statutes and have not kept them. Return
to me, and I will return to you, says the
LORD of hosts. But you say, "How shall
we return?" Will man rob God? Yet
you are robbing me. But you say, "How
are we robbing thee?" In your tithes and
offerings. You are cursed with a
curse, for you are robbing me; the
whole nation of you. Bring the full
tithes into the storehouse, that there
may be food in my house; and thereby
put me to the test, says the LORD of
hosts, if I will not open the windows of
heaven for you and pour down for
you an overflowing blessing.*

Introduction to Malachi

God's people, who were exiled to Babylon, have returned to Judah. They have rebuilt the Temple in Jerusalem. However, the land is still under the authority of a Persian governor when Malachi (about 450 B.C.), in this prophetic book, utters his passionate plea: God's will must be carried out in every detail of living, lest the people forget the lessons learned in the hard years of exile in Babylon.

Malachi, literally "my messenger," uses prose rather than the poetry so common in the prophets. He conveys God's message by a series of questions and answers, which suggest the style of an impatient teacher or an aggressive lawyer.

In chapter 1, verses 1–5, God declares His love for Israel in preference to Edom, her southern neighbor who descended from Esau. Then He denounces Judah's failure to honor the great King, the Lord of Hosts (1:6—2:9).

Malachi condemns the people's flippant attitude toward divorce and toward marriage with people of other faiths (2:10–17). Then God speaks and describes His coming to judge the people for their sorcery, adultery and oppression of the poor (3:1–5). He indicts them for their failure to tithe. Then He promises to "pour down ... an overflowing blessing" if the people test Him by bringing the full tithe into the storehouse (3:6–12). God announces that blessings will be showered on those who serve the Lord but a judgment will be heaped on those who do not.

Malachi's vivid picture of the future includes prophecies of the ministries of the Messiah and His forerunner, Elijah, whom the New Testament identifies as John the Baptist.

Some time ago I heard a good definition of a fool. It came from my teacher, friend, and colleague at Fuller Seminary, Edward John Carnell, who served as president of the Seminary before me. Dr. Carnell told the following story.

Suppose a man's house catches fire, and he rushes around deciding what he should snatch up to take with him as he dashes to safety. His eyes light on his collection of cigar bands, which he has been saving since boyhood days. He tucks them under his arm and gropes his way outside. But in clutching his box of cigar bands he has forgotten his baby, asleep in the crib.

He is guilty of no crime. No charges can be brought against him. No court can convict him. But all the world would call him a fool. When confronted with two possibilities, he chose the lesser. He reached for the cigar bands, not the baby, and showed himself a fool.

To put it another way, he failed to fulfill his responsibility. He acted out of harmony with his own best judgment. His decision clashed with his own definition of good human conduct.

Yet he made that bad decision and had to live with its sting. And a lot of people have done the same. Oh, not in such dramatic form, perhaps, but they have made and are making irresponsible choices. Advances in technology, education, medicine, have made us smarter but not necessarily wiser. Where values are concerned it is not information so much as insight that we need.

Living responsibly means sorting out the higher values from the lower and deliberately sticking with them, especially when it's hard to do so. Modern man has often found it more comfortable to compromise or even forfeit his convictions than to stand by them under pressure. He may not always know what he is doing, and he may not like himself when he does realize what he is doing. But he keeps on doing it.

Not that modern man has a monopoly on irresponsible conduct. It's an agelong human problem. The Hebrew prophet Malachi devotes several chapters to it in the book that closes the Old Testament in our Bible.

Four hundred years before Jesus came to show us true freedom, Malachi talked to his countrymen in stern terms about their lack of responsibility and what it was doing to them. Four of his criticisms point to problems that we face today. Malachi's neighbors were despising God's name, forsaking God's covenant, breaking their marriage vows, and withholding their tithes and offerings. From Malachi's look at the way these issues affected his day we may gain some insight for our own.

Our Responsibility to Honor God's Name

True responsibility begins with a recognition of who God is—His greatness, His power, His authority, His love. Just here, Malachi's people missed the point. They began to take God for granted, to diminish His importance, to ignore His authority.

Malachi's accusation is specific and forceful:

A son honors his father,
and a servant his master.
If then I am a father,
where is my honor?
And if I am a master, where is my fear?
says the LORD of hosts to you,
O priests, who despise my name. . . .

136

When you offer blind animals in sacrifice,
    is that no evil?
And when you offer those that are lame or sick,
    is that no evil?
Present that to your governor; will he
    be pleased with you or show you
       favor? says the LORD of hosts (Mal. 1:6,8).

You remember that the law of God required unblemished animals for sacrifice, the best of the flock. God's people were trying to pawn off on Him their worthless beasts, animals that did them no good, that were probably going to die anyhow. God did not need animals, of course. The cattle on a thousand hills belong to Him. But the animals were a symbol of the esteem in which the people held God, the honor they paid to Him. The sacrifice of animals also showed that the people were truly repentant of their sins. But all this symbolism had been turned sour by their worthless sacrifices.

God's language is strong:

Cursed be the cheat who has a male in
    his flock, and vows it,
and yet sacrifices to the LORD what
    is blemished;
for I am a great King, says the LORD
    of hosts, and my name is feared among the nations (Mal. 1:14).

Cheat is what God calls the man who offers an unfit sacrifice. What would He call us? Animals we don't offer anymore. Jesus' death has made animal sacrifice unnecessary. But we are still obliged to honor God as Father and Master. Nothing in our modern world has made us less dependent on Him or made Him less worthy of our worship and obedience.

Cheats we are if we don't give Him His due—which is our best. Time, money, energy, interest—these we dissipate on lesser enterprises. We laud our astronauts and athletes with an adulation akin to worship. We divide our time between work and leisure with little thought of prayer and service. Church attendance is a casual option which fewer and fewer exercise. God is shut up in the circled holidays on calendars—Thanksgiving, Christmas, Easter—but is not allowed to range through the year as Lord of our daily lives. This a fool's choice, indeed.

Our Responsibility to Keep God's Covenant

To the priests, Malachi, whose name means "my messenger," had a special message to bring. They had failed miserably in their duty to instruct others in the ways of God. And they failed this way despite the unusual blessings God had given them.

My covenant with him [Levi, the ancestor
of the priestly tribe] was a convenant of
life and peace, and I gave them to him,
that he might fear; and he feared me,
he stood in awe of my name. True instruction
was in his mouth, and no wrong was found
on his lips. . . . For the lips of a priest
should guard knowledge, and men should
seek instruction from his mouth, for he is
the messenger of the LORD of hosts.
But you have turned aside from the way;
you have caused many to stumble by your
instruction;

138

you have corrupted the covenant of Levi,
   says the LORD of hosts (Mal. 2:5–8).

Put in simple terms, the priests had broken the contract they had signed with God, a contract that called for them to teach His Law accurately and faithfully. We would be shocked at their failure if it did not remind us sharply of our own. In our day, this side of Pentecost, when God poured out His Spirit on His Church, all Christians are priests (1 Pet. 2:9). As such we have entered into a contract with God to teach the meaning of His ways.

But what has happened? How have we done in our teaching? Have our young people grasped the full meaning of the faith? Are they committed to live by the values revealed in the Bible? Are we as adults trained to solve life's basic puzzles in the way that Jesus and His apostles would have?

Our response to these questions is not an overwhelming yes. Secular thinking has affected us and our children. We have adjusted our values to suit the ways of the world. Our educational systems, both public and private, are conveying attitudes that run counter to God's ways as we find them in the Bible. Sexual experimentation, rejection of authority, disbelief in God's love and power, confidence that all man's problems can be solved by man because he is basically good and simply needs to find himself, encouragement to do what you want to do as long as you feel right about it—these and other attitudes show how far we have departed from the contract that God wants us to keep.

Over our classroom doors and on our kitchen walls and even in some of our Sunday School rooms, Malachi's warning might be inscribed:

But you have turned aside from the way;
    you have caused many to stumble by your
       instruction (Mal. 2:8).

Faced with the choice of God's trustworthy counsel about our sin and His salvation, our conduct and His requirements, or the choice of human wisdom with its glib views of human goodness and power, we have often voted man's way. This is a fool's choice, indeed.

Our Responsibility to Keep Our Marriage Vows

The priests had their compact with God, and they broke it. But the people were no better than the priests. They too had spurned a solemn contract that they should have kept. In judgment, the Lord withheld His blessing from them.

The people were so insensitive to their rebel ways that they asked the prophet Malachi why the Lord refused to bless them. His words left no doubt in their minds:

Because the LORD was witness to the
    covenant between you and the wife of
your youth, to whom you have been faithless,
    though she is your companion and your wife
      by covenant.
Has not the one God made and sustained for us
    the spirit of life? And what does he desire?
Godly offspring. So take heed to yourselves,
    and let none be faithless to the wife of his
      youth.
"For I hate divorce, says the LORD the God
    of Israel, and covering one's garment
with violence, says the LORD of hosts.
    So take heed to yourselves and do not
be faithless" (Mal. 2:14–16).

Whatever else we get from this passage, let one thing be clear: God is interested in your marriage. Yours is not merely a human agreement to be terminated at the whim of either party. California state law permits divorce six months after both parties have testified that their differences cannot be reconciled. But what the law of the state allows, the God of the universe may not approve of. After all, He was witness to vows pronounced "in the sight of God and the presence of these witnesses," as the marriage ceremony reads. Furthermore, He is the true source of "the spirit of life" that draws people together, keeps them alive, and enables them to produce children. Marriage, like all of life, runs on His power. And He has a stake in our marriages, because He is interested in how our children turn out. "Godly offspring" He wants us to have. Unstable homes that laugh at the marriage vows are not a good context in which to raise godly offspring. One of God's purposes in establishing marriage was that we people the earth with men and women that know, obey, and love Him. This was one way of spreading His glory, of honoring His name.

This is not the place to launch a full-scale discussion of a Christian view of marriage and divorce. The issues are complex, and Jesus Himself allows for divorce in extreme cases. But the God-given pattern is one wife, one husband for a lifetime. The roving eye, the flirting hand, the casual dalliance, the passionate affair, the bored fed-upness, the cruel abandonment that we see around and are sometimes tempted to imitate, are not part of God's pattern. To choose one of these rather than faithfulness or loyalty, even at high price, is a fool's choice, indeed.

Our Responsibility to Give God
Our Tithes and Offerings

A society devoid of responsibility needs to learn another thing. Not only do we need to honor God's name, keep His covenant, fulfill our marriage vows, but we need to discharge our responsibility by giving God our tithes and offerings.

If those who offer unfit sacrifices are called *cheats*, those who hold back offerings are called *robbers:*

> Will man rob God?
>> Yet you are robbing me.
> But you say, "How are we robbing thee?"
>> In your tithes and offerings....
> Bring the full tithes into the storehouse,
>> that there may be food in my house;
> and thereby put me to the test,
>> says the LORD of hosts,
> if I will not open the windows of heaven for you
>> and pour down for you an overflowing blessing
>>> (Mal. 3:8,10).

All goods are God's goods. No one else has power to grow crops in the land or deposit minerals in the earth. Whatever we have or use is made from God-given materials. We forget this so easily that God built a reminder into His program for His people—the tithe. A tenth of what they earn or grow or make is to be given to Him, a symbol of their dependence on Him, a token of their gratitude for what He has given.

Many Christians have done well to carry on this practice. People rich and poor can testify that they have gained great satisfaction in giving to God a portion of what they have received. Even in depression days they remained faithful in their tithing. Charles Fuller has told me many times how God's people helped to support and extend his radio ministry even in the depths of the great depression. And our letters today to the joyful sound broadcast tell us that though many people are out of work, or are drawing meager pensions, they take great delight in returning to God part of His gift of goodness to them. To choose to rob God by taking His food, shelter, clothing, and cash without sharing part of it in the causes that honor His name is the fool's choice, indeed.

To live without responsibility is not freedom but foolishness. Malachi's society had to learn that, and so does ours. A friend of mine heard some college students talking about how free they felt now that they were away from the authority of their parents and the responsibilities of their homes. "Why, I'm so free," one young man bragged, "that I haven't brushed my teeth for a week." Foolishness, not freedom, hurting himself and offending others.

We dwellers in a modern world are not above such foolishness and worse. Until we learn to honor the name of our heavenly Father, until we come to follow and teach His ways, until we view marriage as a solemn, binding relationship, until we use our goods for godly purposes, we remain fools, whatever else our accomplishments. In a word we need to catch up with the Bible.

Prayer: Holy Father, preserve us from our own stupidity. Give us wisdom beyond our own. Wisdom to worship, wisdom to obey, wisdom to love, wisdom to give. Through Jesus Christ who taught us true responsibility, we pray. Amen.